LISTEN, MY SON

Listen, My Son

Wisdom for African American Fathers

Lee H. Butler Jr.

Abingdon Press
Nashville

LISTEN, MY SON
WISDOM FOR AFRICAN AMERICAN FATHERS

This book is printed on acid-free paper.

Library of Congress Cataloging-in-Publication Data

Butler, Lee H., 1959-
  Listen, my son : wisdom for African American fathers / Lee H. Butler, Jr.
    p.   cm.
  ISBN 978-0-687-46749-5 (alk. paper)
1. African American fathers—Religious life.   I. Title.
  BR563.N4B89 2010
  248.8′42108996073—dc22

                                                                      2009051669

10 11 12 13 14 15 16 17 18 19—10 9 8 7 6 5 4 3 2 1

MANUFACTURED IN THE UNITED STATES OF AMERICA

To My Grandfathers and Father,
Uncles and Cousins,
and Friends who have
become Brothers

Contents

Contents

PART III: WISDOM FROM FATHERS

Acknowledgments

Writing a book on African American manhood is truly a work-in-process. No man, no matter how old, has all the answers to the question, "What does it mean to be a *real* Black man?" Like all matters of image and identity, this question can only be answered by being in relationship with a community of friends. Without the bond of friendship and respect, the effort to answer the question is likely to be marked by a competition to present the most superior image. I have attempted to answer the question by pointing to the fact that African American manhood is not one image or idea. Black manhood is multidimensional. Furthermore, there are a few key elements that combine to make a real man. Those key elements are the topics for conversation in this book.

I am grateful to Kathy Armistead, editor of this book, for her thoughtfulness in inviting me to reflect and write on this topic. Throughout the writing of this book, she was very encouraging and reflected great patience. Our work together has resulted in a unique book that reflects upon African American manhood through the relational dynamics of fatherhood and mentoring.

In order to put forth my best effort for answering the question of the meaning of real Black manhood, I invited a few friends to have conversation with me on the topic. The more conversations I had, the more convinced I became that I could not address all the concerns alone. As a result, I invited a few friends and colleagues to contribute essays to speak to the different key elements of manhood, each from his own perspective and experience. This book, therefore, is a collaborative effort to encourage African American men to talk with one another about what it means to be Black men in America. So I must thank my friends and colleagues, Professors Horace L. Griffin, Edward P. Wimberly, and Homer U. Ashby Jr., who each contributed chapters to help round out the conversation in the book. In addition, I must give very special thanks to my friend and good brother, Calvin Taylor, who, along with his wife, Toni Taylor, read early drafts of the manuscript and gave me invaluable feedback on my reflections. Calvin is a minister and leader of the Men's Ministry, which includes a boys' rites of passage program, at the Third Baptist Church of Chicago.

I must also thank my family who, from time to time, allowed me to get away to a quiet place where I could write without interruption. A number of friends and colleagues within the Chicago Theological Seminary, the larger academy, and the church regularly encouraged me to complete this book by saying, "This is a word that is so needed." Many friends have shared a hope that I continue to write my analytical reflections by saying things like, "Your books should be as numerous as the branches of a plant." Without the support and encouragement of family and friends, thought would never reach the printed page. Thank you one and all!

Introduction

While having coffee with a dear friend and colleague, I shared that I was writing about African American men. I let him know this book will explore African American manhood through the lens of fatherhood and the relationships African American fathers have with their children. Without further elaboration on this theme, my friend, who is European American, asked the question, "Is there a difference?" He, knowing that there is something different, yet not wanting to immediately concede the differences, went on to ask whether European American men and African American men who are fathers are actually doing anything different with our children. My instinctual response was to say, "Of course there will be great similarities. We are both human and love our children. The differences will be in the social factors that affect our relationships with our children." I continued by sharing my concerns and described my passion for this book. I explained what I believed to be the most important issues that would become the heart of this book. Ultimately, I stated that European American men and African American men face different social stressors that affect our manhood and therefore influence the ways we each prepare our children to live healthy and productive lives. My friend did not disagree.

Living in an era where we want to believe that all Americans have truly been created equal, that we have been endowed by our Creator with the same inalienable rights, we want to believe that "manhood is manhood" and "fatherhood is fatherhood" in America. For indeed, every father in America dreams of providing his children the best that life has to offer. We all want to present our children with good gifts. We want to provide our children with the feeling of security that there is someone they can depend on as their protector, keeping watch over them while they sleep. We want to ensure that our children have more than enough food, clothing, and happy experiences that offer them great joy and laughter. Every father wants to provide his children with a quality education and inspire a self-esteem that allows his children to believe that they can do anything and everything they aspire to do. So as my friend and I began to explore his question about whether there is a difference, we agreed that fundamentally we both want the same things for our children; and yet there are aspects of American culture that influence how we relate to our children and suggest the possibilities we have in America. If we live and conduct ourselves as though there is no difference, we live behind a veil that distorts our vision and does not prepare our children—our sons and our daughters—to confront the harsh realities of American life.

Living without a Veil

What is the meaning of African American Christian manhood in the new millennium? The former images that articulated manhood were deeply imprinted by efforts to counter white supremacy's ideologies. The legacy of slavery and the psychic legacy of social and physical emasculation resulted in reconstructive efforts to restore African American men to their identified proper place within the family and society as fathers and heads of the households. This has been the ministry focus within many African American congregations. The reclamation of the African American family has largely meant the restoration of the patriarchal male. As important as a restorative effort is, the images of father and head of household have been motivated by the central themes of male dominance and male sexual prowess. Even as we have longed to counter white supremacist ideologies of Black manhood, we have tended to develop reconstructive efforts based on the very images that have been used to oppress our humanity as men of African descent.

I believe it is time to take a fresh look at African American manhood. It is time to look at all the factors that have encouraged and denigrated the lives of African American men. This book is an effort to explore the factors that influence the relationships that Black men have with one another and the ways our self-understanding affects and influences our children and the life of the community. We must move beyond the solution that teaching manhood is only about mentoring boys to become men. We must move beyond the brutality of homophobia that victimizes Black gay men. We must also challenge the popular paradigm that considers the social qualification for manhood to be fatherhood. Included in this social qualification is the idea that the man must father a son. "True" fatherhood—and by extension true manhood—is far more than siring a son. If sons are the basic measure of a man, what happens to our senses of self, to our feelings about family name, when we only father daughters? Furthermore, what happens to our senses of self when we become fathers to gay sons? These are questions we simply must talk about with one another.

We, African American men, have often been devastated by our feelings related to fatherhood, feelings that have regularly led us to be painfully abusive to one another and to women and daughters while encouraging boys and sons to be disrespectful and irresponsible in their relationships with women and girls. My hope is that redefining manhood through reimagining mentoring and fatherhood will improve the quality of our lives as Black men. By broadening our understanding of the enduring images that inform and guide African American manhood, I hope to inspire a new vision for the future of the African American community. Through a nontraditional exploration of the themes of boys, men, fathers, sons, and daughters, I hope to transform a Black ministry focus that supports the supremacy-prescribed images of male dominance and sexual prowess as a foundation of manhood into a healthier, more relational ministry focus that is truly family and community affirming.

Chapter Overview

This book has been written to promote a series of conversations that are extremely important for African American men to have with one another. Although it is not necessary for everyone to agree with my opinions, I hope everyone will agree to the importance of having an open conversation on the ideas I present for discussion. I have tried to present the issues as directly as I can. At times, the language will seem to fall just short of "locker room" talk. Locker room talk, although sometimes crass, is a limited conversation among very few men. And although usually less crass, the same would be true of barbershop talk. But church talk tends to be the least direct of all. If, however, we cannot bring our most direct conversations to the household of faith, then our attempts to live faithful lives as men become dishonest activities devoted to looking good.

This book is grounded in the hope of encouraging a larger, more sustained conversation among more African American men. If we cannot bring the boasts of the locker room and the challenge of the barbershop to the meeting room at the church, we will not take the next step in the reformation of our being as faithful men of African descent. As a result, I say throughout the book, "Let's talk." The organization of the book invites conversations in three areas of our lives for considering our manhood and relationships. In part 1, I invite us to take a close look at and talk about the relationships of fathers and sons. In part 2, the focus is on fathers and daughters. And in part 3, I encourage us to gather the wisdom of our experience by talking about the images we consider to be reflective of our very best selves. The three areas of consideration have been further divided into eight chapters, each chapter raising a different concern. Nevertheless, every concern connects one concern to another. Also, colleagues in pastoral care have written several chapters.

Chapter 1 is an examination of our overall social context and looks at the issues that surround boys growing into men. Chapter 2 explores the relationship that men direct to boys and what it means to become a father. Chapter 3 encourages us to look at the relationship between men, boys, and mentoring. Chapter 4, written by Dr. Horace Griffin, identifies the importance of talking about our gay sons and the impact of being gay on our understanding of manhood. Chapter 5, written by Dr. Edward Wimberly, explores the dynamics of the birth of girls on our self-image as Black men. Chapter 6, written by Dr. Homer Ashby Jr., encourages us to be responsible for the care and nurture of our daughters. Chapter 7 invites us to talk about the unhealthy ways we have seen and continue to treat girls and women as property. Chapter 8 identifies the role models and images that will help us take the next step in our journey toward becoming healthier men who are committed to one another, family, and community.

PART I

Lessons from Fathers to Sons

CHAPTER ONE

Boys to Men: Growing into African American Manhood

Let's have a conversation. Let's talk man to man and brother to brother. Let's talk about how we grow into adults and what manhood means. Let's talk brother to brother and man to man about how we relate to one another as we grow into adults. Let's talk about what defines our maleness and our manhood. Let's talk brother to brother as African American men. Let's talk openly and honestly about what it means to be Black men and American. We can no longer assume that we all know what it means to be African American men. This is a conversation that is long overdue. Let's talk together and listen to one another. This is our time to talk instead of being talked about. It is time for us to shed the unhealthy images and opinions that we have accepted as the standards of what it means to be Black men. The benefits of our talk will transform our souls as well as benefit all the girls and women in our lives.

Although this will be a conversation that girls and women will be able to eavesdrop on, this is really our conversation. This is a "FUBU" meeting—that is, this is a conversation "for us by us," with lifesaving implications. In the absence of having this open, heartfelt conversation with one another, we will continue to define ourselves according to stereotypes and legends. It is absolutely essential that we define ourselves and our future. If we refuse to have the conversation that clarifies who we are once and for all, we will continue to be misrepresented, inappropriately defined, and inaccurately described. We will continue to be labeled an endangered species whose being has been characterized as a brute, as an animal, as a less-than-human beast that prowls American society. So, let's talk together, brothers.

Framing the Conversation

The roots of Black survival are found in the bonds of family ties and in the safety and sanctity of the community. Our lives in America have been challenged for generations by hardships that we have only been able to overcome by pulling together and supporting one another. We have continuously worked to inspire one another to embrace life by pulling together and blessing one another. We have not always been as good to one another as we should have been, but through it all we have maintained a forward-looking hopefulness. Deep within us there has resided a message that says, "United we stand; divided we die." This message has stimulated our resistance and nurtured our will to live. As the African American community hopes to look beyond survival by envisioning the future growth and fruit of African American life, few issues are as critical or as difficult to talk about as the roles of Black men to the health and well-being of the African American family and community.

A review of the status of men within American society leaves no question: the United States of America is a male-preferred society. Given this fact, we should not think to minimize the importance of men to the maintenance of family bonds and the sanctity of the community. To the contrary, we must explore the ways men can play a more productive role within the family and community. Men must actively participate in cultivating and nurturing relationships that support life and encourage mutuality. This being the case, the contributions of African American men to the overall well-being of the family and community are more important than many of the critics of patriarchy would lead most to believe. Although our roles have been variously described in psychology, sociology, history, educational theories, and theater—both positively and negatively—the role and image of African American manhood is far more socially and emotionally complex than the bulk of the literature and theatrical presentations have managed to express. Too often we are stereotyped and critiqued by comparing us unfairly to others. Many theories, images, and norms regarding what it means to be a man in America have been developed by identifying Black men as the negative example. Consider, for instance, that the image of manhood in America was the plantation owner. He made his living by exploiting enslaved Africans. The plantation overseer sought to live by the image of the plantation owner, so he victimized enslaved Africans. Neither the landowner nor the overseer considered African men as having the potential of matching them in manhood. Consequently, to encourage African American men to conform to the ideals we were never intended to live into only makes our lives more painful. We must, therefore, speak for ourselves to say who we are and to define the meaning of healthy relationships that will preserve the integrity of our families and community.

Because the African American identity is largely grounded in family and community, to approach the issue of African American manhood with an individualistic understanding would be an error. We need to be able to talk about what it means to be Black men, without the burden of being judged according to standards set by other racial-ethnic communities. We need to be able to talk freely and openly about who we want to be, about who we need to be, and about who we can be—with God's help. We must begin to talk about promoting ways of being that will help us maintain our traditional commitments to family and community while at the same time not encouraging us to evaluate our future based on individualistic models of living. Let me be very clear at this point in the conversation: talking about Black manhood by focusing on the importance of fatherhood *is not* the same as advocating the biological function of making babies. To the contrary, I am advocating responsibility and leadership as important attributes of fatherhood that must be lived within the family and community. Embracing the vital attributes of fatherhood as the best way to live out our manhood is what I am encouraging through this conversation.

Without a doubt, there has been an overwhelmingly negative way of understanding the experience of Black manhood and how that experience relates to fatherhood in the United States. While fatherhood has been one of the defining features of manhood, once the youth has sired a child, which unfortunately often identifies him as a man, the fullest definitions of fatherhood cease to exert any influence upon the defining features of Black manhood.

Distorting the responsibilities of fatherhood will ultimately distort the image of manhood. This has been a real problem for African American life. The irony is there are moments when the African American church supports the distortion. We must end the distortions that are often based on inappropriate comparisons and speak for ourselves on the best ways to support and advance the community.

By way of example, it is a well-known fact that fathers play a distinctive and vital role in the identity formation of children. Also, a person's relationship with his or her father is as important to a person's psychospiritual health as a relationship with one's mother. If we do not have positive images for guiding this relationship, we will condemn our community to destruction by destroying the healthy images that nurture our growth. We should not deceive ourselves by believing that all the images presented by the church are positive images that will nurture our relationships. Even in the church we can see varying dynamics played out in the ways we talk about God as Father and Jesus as Man—and both beings often understood as white. Many of those among us who would argue that God does not care about black and white have a hard time imagining God or Jesus looking like anything other than the most popular white images of God and Jesus. The language of the Black church and our experience as Americans combine to create a very complicated picture of African American manhood. If we are not sensitive to the full range of meanings contained within the Christian images of manhood, we run the risk of participating in the psychospiritual denigration and emasculation of men that is so socially pervasive.

Manhood in the United States

Manhood in America, as an idea, is continuously reviewed and revised. It is constantly being scrutinized and modified as the nation continues to address a long history of male preference within American culture. This means that the domineering attitudes about manhood are steadily being challenged and adjusted with the hope of bringing about a more equitable society with more balance in all of our relationships. Undoubtedly, a review of manhood in American culture applies to all men; but we must also accept that in the history of American society, all men were not created equal under the law. Clearly there is a strong history of African American men being denied the social privileges of manhood by both written and unwritten laws.

African American men have regularly been denied access to the jobs and social mobility afforded European American men. All the sayings that describe the responsibilities of manhood and fatherhood within American society, such as "Pull yourself up by your own bootstraps," have hurt rather than helped most African American men. Too many problematic conditions that have been constructed by white supremacy have denied African American men the resources to acquire the "boots" that would allow upward mobility. In too many instances, social conditions have forced African American men into the degraded position of being "boot lickers" instead of wearing boots like other men. Time and time again, studies and documentaries have revealed that as African American men we suffer the stigma of being viewed as though we are all criminals in the eyes of white America. The perception of African American men as criminal is always a matter of skin color before it ever becomes a matter of legal record. This criminalizing attitude that is directed against us was restated with supporting research and statistics in the 2008 CNN documentary *Black in America*, with Soledad O'Brien. The series from start to finish gave witness to the fact that Black boys and men are regularly viewed as being irresponsible and socially uncontrollable. The series stated that forces within America regularly stigmatize us.

The developmental movement from boys to men generally reflects a movement from social irresponsibility to social responsibility. In the United States, this movement has been determined by age and rites of passage. The Christian Scriptures have promoted twelve years old as the age of responsibility, and the American law of the land has attributed responsibility to individuals at eighteen years and twenty-one years of age. Both Christian Scripture and American society have rituals that mark the transition from boys to men. Whereas we tend to regard twelve years old as the age for showing Christian responsibility through baptism or confirmation into church membership, American social responsibility has a two-part rite of passage into the responsibilities of adulthood that are marked by education, graduation, and chronology. At eighteen years of age one tends to graduate from high school, which marks the beginning of adult life; and at twenty-one years of age a person crosses over into the legal age for full adult privileges and responsibilities.

The American educational system has been a significant institution for making citizens for the nation. Unfortunately, the system does not always cultivate the best within us to become all we can be. Quite often, the system tracks students into certain paths in order to establish a certain social order. How many times have you heard of a teacher or school counselor encouraging an African American student to underachieve in the selection of her or his career path and to call the path of underachievement realistic? Perhaps you were one of those students who was told you should choose a trade instead of college, or choose a community college instead of aspiring to a top-tier college or university. I am not being critical of trade schools or community colleges. I am being critical of the influences within the educational system that promote underachievement among African Americans. I am critical of a system that grades skin color and not the true quality of schoolwork. This encouragement of underachievement is often directed most sharply against African American boys and young men. Tracking African American boys toward underachievement is one of the ways the system has sought to make us irresponsible, with poor attitudes toward citizenship. Let's look more carefully at the message and process.

Eighteen and Twenty-one

Eighteen is the age of transition from one's home of origin to the establishment of a new home. The rite of passage that marks this transition is high school graduation. It is not unusual to hear the parenting statement, "Once you graduate, you are on your own!" Yet, with so many African American men now dropping out of high school, many are not experiencing that particular socially accepted rite of passage. In this instance, going out "on your own" is not marked by a celebration. This moment of transition is marked by failure and disappointment. Not graduating from high school in effect reinforces the socially inferior status of African American males as being boys in this society because they have not been initiated by the first part of the two-part rite of passage into American manhood.

Twenty-one is the age of full adulthood as one completes trade school and apprenticeship or graduates from college to begin full participation in the workforce as a responsible citizen who is now expected to start his own family. Becoming a blue-collar professional or a white-collar professional ensures one's ability to be the provider one is expected to be as a man. Although the picture of the household has changed, we are still socialized to see the man as the head of the household providing for the financial security of the family. The primary challenge here is that, whereas a high school diploma once meant that one would only obtain an entry-level position, the current experience of many African American men is that a college diploma now carries the same meaning and weight that a high school diploma once did. It only ensures an entry-level labor position. This is a poor incentive for encouraging Black men to go to college. Furthermore, with many unionized trades having color as a workman's criteria, and many African American men not entering or not graduating from college, many African American men have not been initiated by the second of the two-part rite of passage into American manhood.

Making a Man

Carter G. Woodson wrote a book in 1933 entitled *The Mis-Education of the Negro*. Woodson's thesis stated that America's educational system sought to indoctrinate African Americans to accept an inferior position within American society in the same way the Middle Passage sought to brainwash free Africans to accept slavery. Because education is supposed to lead a person through a process of self-discovery—that is, to learn who one truly is on the inside and where one comes from—Woodson said that African Americans were miseducated. We were being directed away from the true educational path of knowledge and self-discovery. Instead of being educated into the knowledge of who we are, we were being miseducated into accepting inappropriate identities. While the American educational system sought to educate one group, the same system was directed to "train" African Americans to be underachievers and to accept an unequal status in life.

Historically, becoming a blue-collar skilled laborer was the normal route for establishing a home. While African American women were socialized to become domestics, schoolteachers, and nurses, African American men were socialized to become sanitation workers, craftsmen, and nonskilled laborers. For a long time it was the extraordinary Black man who had the opportunity to achieve white-collar success after college. Over time, women's opportunities increased while men's opportunities went into decline. And so there are more African American women in white-collar professional positions, with African American men struggling to break the sexualized color line.

Employment, more specifically the work that one does, is a primary influence on how every person understands himself or herself. People tend to identify themselves by the jobs they hold, and speak their life's meaning in this world by the work they do. If African Americans have been relegated to the lowest, most menial jobs available, the system has ascribed the lowest meaning and value to our being. In order for African American men to know a high level of self-esteem and value, we cannot have our self-esteem rooted in our labor. We must ground our being in ideas more soulful than the work we do and the money we earn. If our sense of self-worth is grounded in economics, and the economic system is directed toward benefiting someone other than Black men, then we cannot yield to the economic system that has been dedicated to miseducating us. We must not accept the idea that we are inferior beings!

Black Boys

Generations of African American men have been assigned the status of boys even when they were well advanced in years. The term *boys* can be an endearing term that describes the bonds of friendship. When the term was applied to African American men as a collective, it had a negative and derogatory meaning. It referred to a social status rather than an acknowledgment of the bonds of friendship. Declaring African American men to be boys not only identified us as irresponsible; the identification also alleged that we were incapable of managing ourselves. To refer to a full-grown African American man as a "boy" is to identify him as an infantile, irresponsible person who needs constant supervision. When non–African Americans addressed African American men as "boy," the label was stressing the inferior status that African American males held within society. Linking this understanding with the educational system, if we have not experienced the two-part rite of passage into American adulthood there is little else within American society that transitions us from boys to men.

Being outside the educational rite of passage has often resulted in new rites being established to mark the transition from boys to men. The most common rite, which has often reinforced the view that we are irresponsible, has been fatherhood. Whereas sex with multiple partners has been a point of pride and not simply a matter of physical pleasure, being able to say that there are children from one's loins has been a status symbol among men. Because so much has been done to encourage irresponsibility by the larger American society, it is essential that we make a distinction between sirehood and fatherhood. When I say "sirehood," I am referring to the procreative act that results in the birth of a child. This is to be distinguished from "fatherhood," which means the man has accepted full responsibility for the growth, nurture, and development of his daughter(s) and son(s). A boy who sires a child often has no clue about how to be a father. This is especially problematic when sirehood becomes the rite of passage that transitions boys to men. If the boy has no interest in or knowledge of fatherhood, the newborn child is left vulnerable unless other systems of male nurturing are developed for the child.

It is well known historically for an African American man to be called "boy"; the intention being, as I have already said, to identify him as infantile and irresponsible. Labeling a Black man "boy" not only denies his manhood, it also denigrates his identity and suggests that he has no integrity. And why? All because someone else has the need to feel superior and more important. But what does this mean for the one who, in terms of age, is in fact a boy? Boys are socialized from birth to be independent, aggressive, and assertive. These qualities are generally seen as being positive for boys and are considered the building blocks for manhood. However, when preadolescent boys express these positive qualities, they tend to be seen as negative qualities. Independent, aggressive, assertive Black boys tend to be seen as troubled problem children. The Black boy, then, is given two confusing and contradictory messages. One message says being aggressive is good. The other message says being aggressive is bad. The double message to Black boys begins to build a double-consciousness very early in life. Black boys learn, sometimes as early as preschool, that they live life beneath a double standard. They learn that there are rules for social engagement that are not applied equally. The major confusion of the double standard is this: even if they follow both rules to the letter of the law, they do not reap the benefits of social acceptance. In the absence of a positive image of Black manhood and an affirming rite-of-passage process, boys will embrace all the negativity they learn as a result of the social rejection they experience. This condition becomes the seeds of rage that Black men know very well.

Rage, Sex, and the Gun

Rage is the deep, all-consuming energy that resides within. It is anger at its extreme. Think of it this way: if anger is a heavy rain, then rage is a Category 5 hurricane! Rage tends to have nothing to do with hatred. Rage is the explosive release of energy that results in destruction because it has been held in and pressed down for too long. Rage is the volcano that erupts because the lava can no longer be contained underground. Just as the lava defies gravity as it shoots into the air, exploding rage is defiance against years of frustration, suppressed anger, unfair treatment, and abuse. Rage does not have a sense of morality; it does not distinguish between right and wrong. Rage is that moment when a person just snaps! He is in a daze and does not have awareness until the smoke from the explosion clears. Then he is able to see what he has just done. After rage expresses itself, his moral development determines whether he cares about the destruction of his explosion or not.

African American boys are shown sex and the gun as resources for managing rage. Of course, they are given sports too; but for the conflicts sports cannot settle, sex and the gun will. Sex and the gun are tools of initiation as boys seek to develop into men. Engaging in sex and shooting the gun are often understood to be the acts that get a boy the respect he desires. Yet, in many ways, how different are the shots fired from an orgasm from those fired from the gun for one who desires respect? The type of respect that is usually desired tends to be a respect associated with responsibility—a respect that should only be reserved and given to men. But, for many boys, sex and the gun become the pathway to manhood. Unfortunately, this definition of manhood has been directed by rage. And given that rage is a destructive force, this definition of manhood creates destructive boys who believe themselves to be men. They earn their sense of respect through acts of violence. Any challenge to the destructive energy that guides their lives is seen as a challenge to their manhood, which cannot be tolerated. This challenge of manhood usually ends in sexual violence or gun violence.

Rape, although the best known, is not the only form of sexual violence. When a guy treats a girl or woman as nothing more than a piece of meat wrapped around his manliness, it can be just as violent to her being as rape. When sexual intercourse is only about his lustful desires, then he has done violence to her being as a divinely beautiful creation. A sexual encounter that has been directed by lust is emotionally empty. It is aggression without sharing and only uses her as "target practice." His lack of care is a violence that reduces her to something less than human—in much the same way many in American society see him. In his act of sexual violence he rapes himself of human passion and dignity by his violation of another.

A boy's first sexual encounter is identified as another important rite of passage for his transition into manhood. In many ways, the girl he has sex with for his first experience is less important than having that first sexual encounter. Having sex—and reporting having had sex—initiates him into the circle of male power. I remember being told as a boy that having sex made guys better in sports. So the best athletes were thought to have sex all the time. Men continue to believe this myth as we view the personal lives of male professional athletes. We want to know about the professional athlete's "game" on and off the field or court. After a boy's first sexual experience, continuing to have sex and who he has sex with become more important as a way of continuing to prove and affirm his manhood. Similarly, pulling the trigger of a gun for the first time is what matters, be it the random shooting of an innocent passerby or a drive-by shooting. After the first time, the person he shoots and the reasons for shooting promote the shooter's status in the ranks of the circle of male power. Furthermore, he must continue to shoot or he may be suspected of having "gone soft," like being sexually impotent.

Once he has been initiated, sex and the gun become his way of life. Every man knows that severe anxiety or fear will result in a lack of sexual response. For both sex and the gun, responsiveness is the standard for measuring manhood. He has to be "hard." If he is thought to be "limp" and unable to shoot, he is seen as power-less. If he cannot prove that he is hard, he becomes unworthy to be called a man and becomes a target himself. So he shoots sexually and with the gun. This way of seeing life also suggests that he has surrendered to the rage within. He becomes the predator that soci-ety wants to believe is the core of his being. He constantly prowls to satisfy the deep, all-consuming rage that directs his every look. Whether shooting through sex or shooting with the gun, he needs to feel the power of the explosion that says he is a force to be reck-oned with. But to the extent that both sex and the gun are expres-sions of rage, he destroys himself with each encounter in the same way he sees the life of his target as insignificant.

Turning the Negative into a Positive

The long and negative history of America seeking to dominate Black males must be renegotiated if Black boys are to mature into Black men. For as much as the immature, irresponsible image of a Black boy is the central image for making a man in America, trans-forming the negativity of the image into a positive is essential. The image of "Black boy" is regularly used to instruct one group as a way of saying, "This is what you must avoid being like," while another group is tracked to become the image, imprisoning them into an unavoidable pit of social despair. Boy and sirehood are a large part of our psychic legacy. And as much as we might debate the power of the Black-boy image today, I believe it continues to influence our self-understanding as Black men in America.

I compare the power of the image of "Black boy" to that of the American dream. The negative image of the Black boy is influential in the same way the American dream continues to influence all Americans in powerful ways. It does not matter that the dream has been described and redefined over and over again as a powerful social motivator; the dream continues to be experienced by countless African Americans as a social inhibitor and nightmare. In 2005, the Senate apologized to the nation and African Americans for failing to pass antilynching laws. Lynching was a brutal and vicious assault on African American manhood that often included castration as part of the ritualized sacrifice of the Black male body. On July 29, 2008, the House of Representatives passed House Resolution 194, which apologized for the enslavement and racial segregation of African Americans. Efforts to pass a resolution of apology for slavery have stumbled and stalled largely over the issue of reparations. The apology, however, does acknowledge that African Americans have not had equal access and opportunity to participate in the American dream. The passing of this resolution makes it clear that Black men have not been afforded the same privilege of living as other American men under the law. Again, we have lived with legislated and de facto "boyhood."

Over the centuries, we have continued to struggle to redefine ourselves as Black American men. The language of the American dream defines and describes the benefits due to each and every American man. Yet, just as there has been a double message around the language of "boy," there has been a double message regarding the American work ethic. And with work being an important part of self-identity, the inability to live the dream by being locked out of employment that could lead to upward mobility has again meant that manhood has had to be grounded in a soulfulness that has not been dependent upon the dream, work, and money. Unfortunately, these are important sources for defining American life and manhood in America.

Although we no longer hear African American men labeled as "boy" in most public conversations, as we did in the 1960s and earlier, that history continues to be extremely influential. Rather than speaking the label, "boy" is the label placed on our being through gestures and attitudes. The negativity associated with being an African American man is regularly reinforced by society at large. Each and every day, popular culture presents African American men as boys to be feared. With this as the case, it is very appropriate to reimage the journey from boys to men. It is not just the physical journey that needs to be reimaged; it is also the spiritual journey from boyhood and sirehood to manhood and fatherhood that promotes living a life of meaningful relationships and responsibility.

Biblical Character Study

To explore these dynamics, let us consider the life and times of Ishmael, son of Abraham and Hagar. As I wrote in my first book, *A Loving Home*, insights into our spiritual deliverance as men of African descent are contained in the story of Ishmael. It is true that the Christian heritage focuses on Isaac as the son of promise and blessing. It is also true that in the larger story of Ishmael's life his descendants became the followers of Islam. To suggest that we seek to gain clarity on our own spiritual journey through identifying with Ishmael is not to suggest that we ought to be Muslims. However, understanding Ishmael's story can help us understand our challenges as Black men in America because our story, as men of African descent, is closer to Ishmael's experience than it is to Isaac's experience. Ishmael's story is our story.

There are many Bible stories we can learn from as African American men, but few stories are as striking as a mirror of our experience as Ishmael's story. Ishmael was of African descent. Black men in America are of African descent. Ishmael was the son of an enslaved African woman. Likewise, an important part of our story in America is that of being the sons of enslaved Africans. Ishmael was marked as being socially unacceptable. He was described as being "a wild ass of a man" (Gen. 16:12). We have been similarly described as socially unacceptable wild animals. Ishmael's play has been interpreted as rough and aggressive. Black boys have also regularly been described as aggressive and violent. And just as Ishmael was rejected and outcast from Abraham's household and denied an inheritance, we African American men have often been the rejected and outcast sons of America. For generations we have been denied our slice of the American pie. Ishmael's story is actually more closely related to our own story than to Isaac's story.

Ishmael was the firstborn of Abraham. We generally assume that a son, particularly a firstborn son, would be the delight of his father's eye. He probably was for a short period of time. But then Ishmael was rejected at the time when he would have looked to his father for guidance on what it means to grow into manhood. The great tragedy is the very poor example Abraham set as the image and model of manhood and fatherhood. As a boy, Ishmael learned that mothers—not fathers—look out for and protect their sons. Both Sarah and Hagar acted on behalf of their boys. Abraham did not. Abraham's abandonment of his son, therefore, encouraged Ishmael to be less trusting of and less relationally connected to other men. He was victimized and traumatized by being denied what he was most entitled to: a loving, caring, present father. Furthermore, he was sent away to die in the wilderness with his mother, who was also victimized and traumatized by Abraham. With this experience of rejection, betrayal, and abandonment, it is not surprising that Ishmael would become "a wild ass of a man." He was at war with Abraham's fatherly decisions and with himself as he struggled to grow into manhood.

Ishmael's lack of relationship with Abraham provoked his own experiences with rage, sex, and the gun. Looking at those dynamics in the context of his life and times, the circumstances of his life no doubt produced deep resentment and rage. Who can be rejected, abandoned, and sentenced to death and not have a deep emotional reaction? I have no doubt that Ishmael was filled with rage over the treatment he received from his father. The story includes a statement that Hagar found a wife for Ishmael from among the Egyptians. And while we know nothing of his handling of sex, we do know that he sired twelve sons. He became a great nation through his descendants. Was sex an expression of love or was it a weapon for Ishmael? As a wild ass of a man at war with all, I venture to say that he also used sex as a weapon, unless he received good mentoring from the men of Egypt. The text is clear to say, however, that Ishmael became a hunter who was very proficient with the bow and arrow, the gun of his day. I believe this description speaks directly to a very guarded way of living in the world. Being proficient with a bow and arrow means that one does not have to be near one's prey to kill. If a bow is power, and killing is a sign of manhood, then this is a statement that Ishmael became a mighty man.

I hope that we are better able to see the challenges we face as we progress from boyhood to manhood through a review of Ishmael's story. Imagine how different Ishmael's life might have been if Abraham had been a better father and role model. Let us strive to be and do what Abraham was unable to be and do in Ishmael's life.

CHAPTER TWO

Men to Boys: Affirming African American Fatherhood

Continuing our conversation, let's talk about African American men and the meaning of fatherhood. Let's talk, not just about African American men becoming fathers, but also about the significance of African American men becoming fathers of sons. In later chapters, we will talk about African American men becoming fathers of daughters. For now, let's talk about how fathers relate to sons, and how men relate to boys. Let's talk about what a man gives to his son, and what his son gives him in return. Because our most significant image of manhood is fatherhood, we run the risk of abusing our children for the sake of establishing our own self-esteem. Abusing one another is exactly what we want to end. Just as our conversation on boys to men encouraged the importance of discovering a soulful ground for our being, the social relationship from men to boys requires a spiritual image. So let's talk about fathers supporting sons, and men supporting boys.

Becoming a Father

Because the United States is a male-preferred society, an incredible emphasis is placed upon sirehood and the procreation of sons. Physical power and prowess are two elements associated with popular definitions of manhood. A "real man" is thought to be aggressive and assertive. The image of the real man is a media icon that has been posted far and wide. This male-preferred society communicates that you always know a real man when you see him. Furthermore, his image is so distinctive you also know if you

19

are a real man by comparing yourself to his image. The image of the real man declares he knows how to use his power and prowess to get everything he wants. The image projects the idea that a real man has the power and prowess to physically dominate. This, in turn, is joined with the procreative power and prowess to impregnate. The two understandings of power and prowess give instruction and direction to male activities. The basic image of manhood encourages attitudes that say a man is a superior being.

Sirehood is a popular rite of passage that inappropriately identifies manhood. It is a peculiar phenomenon whereby a boy who sires a child is immediately transitioned by his peers into the status of manhood. In those instances, fatherhood, which requires love and responsibility, is rarely a consideration. Those who understand sirehood to be the mark of manhood reduce us to being a physical shell without heart or soul. To the extent that procreation passes physical attributes through DNA, soulless procreation passes a legacy of spiritual disconnection. This means before birth the child is abandoned by an attitude that boasts of the evidence of manhood instead of celebrating the blessing of a child. Sirehood is irresponsible and selfish. Sirehood makes a boy into a spiritual orphan longing for a relationship with a man-child incapable of sharing his life. This is why mentoring is extremely important. Mentoring will help mature the sire into a father, and in those instances where a boy's sire is completely unavailable, his mentor can become his father figure and spiritual guide through life.

She's Pregnant!

Boys and men experience many different feelings when their partners make the announcement, "I'm pregnant." Depending on what the man or boy was expecting as the result of engaging in the act of procreation, he will be extremely happy, unaffected, annoyed, or sad. If he is an expectant father, he lives with a sense of responsibility and anticipation in life. The expectant father is generally made happy by the announcement of new life. He knows life is larger than himself and that the power of life is greater than his own power. Although there are instances when an expectant father may be saddened by the timing, his reverence for life and his experience of having been nurtured in love gives him the heart to adjust and prepare himself and his surroundings for the life that is to come.

If the act of procreation was nothing more than an act of lust for immediate and selfish pleasure, the expectant sire will be unaffected or annoyed. If the expectant sire never made an emotional and intimate connection with his partner, he will be completely unaffected. His lack of feeling is evidence of his selfish interest in his own physical gratification. If his partner was nothing more than the temporary object of his desire, her sharing the news might annoy him. His annoyance results from his feeling of resentment for what he considers to be an intrusion on his gratification. It disrupts his good feeling. To his mind, she had the nerve to try and make him responsible for what he never considered to be an act of responsibility. He got what he wanted, so nothing else matters. Furthermore, he could also conclude: "She got what she wanted. If she didn't want a baby, she should have taken care of that before she got with me. That's all on her!"

The selfishness of sirehood is socially conditioned. Boys are regularly taught to depend on no one except themselves. They are taught to trust only in their own power and prowess. To the extent that boys have been socialized to be independent, taking responsibility for another does not always connect to their reasoning. One might think that sports is an area of socialization that promotes support through teamwork. But even teamwork is a collaboration of individuals. The whole notion of teamwork says that everyone depends on one another in order to win. Although there are pithy phrases like "There is no 'I' in team," a winning team tends to depend on individual performance. Teamwork says that we each have a job and everyone must do his job for the team to win. When someone is not doing his job, it is often thought that a poor performance affects other individual performances and brings down the team. And if the team loses, more often than not there tends to be finger-pointing to individuals who lost the game, rather than pointing out a team's collective performance.

Sirehood is actually no different from a sporting event. Winning is based on individual performance. The sire's partner is seen as different—an opponent rather than a teammate. She is someone or something to be conquered for the glory of winning. She is to be conquered as a symbol of his power, prowess, and dominance. In sports, if you hurt your opponent on the field, you are not encouraged to care for him if it is a serious injury. He is socialized to say, "That's part of the game. Deal with it or stay off the field." Within the sire's way of seeing things, his partner is supposed to take care of herself in the same independent way he takes care of himself. His selfishness says, "Since she was dumb enough to get pregnant, she needs to handle her business."

When boys receive the appropriate mentoring and preparation for manhood, fatherhood becomes a celebration of life and love. Boys who have been prepared for manhood know the difference between lust and love. Their values are grounded in such a way that they feel the difference between sirehood and fatherhood. This does not mean that mentored boys will not engage in sex. What it does mean is boys who have been mentored for manhood have the internal resources to rise to the occasion and assume the responsibilities given to fatherhood.

Delivery and Announcement

The birth of a child gives voice to male pride, even among many men who have no intention of fathering. There are pats on the back and acts of celebration and pride. Sometimes the new dad presents gifts to others. The classic cigar, as a symbol of accomplishment, is sometimes given to celebrate the new birth. There are cheap cigars specifically designed for the occasion as well as bubble gum cigars for those who want to give the token symbolically. Announcing the birth of a child is one of the many proud moments a man can experience as a father.

Although there is great pride expressed at the birth of a child, there tends to be more pride in announcing the birth of a son than there is in announcing the birth of a daughter. Even if a man proudly announces the birth of a daughter, he tends not to be given the same social status or stature as the man who announces the birth of a son. A son is regarded as a reflection of manhood. Sadly, a daughter does not affirm his image within society in the same way. A son's actions his whole life through are always a reflection back to his father. A daughter will reflect a close and special relationship with her father, but a son expresses the measure of a man in this society. These same dynamics are also reflected in our spiritual understandings. We tend to see the relationship between God and humanity functioning the same way. Adam and men are seen as the image of God, while Eve and women tend to be seen as the subordinates of Adam and men. We tend to declare the power of God in the lives and activities of men, and women tend to only be given honor through their association with men rather than their association with God. Consequently, men of God have been exalted above women of God; and sons have been exalted above daughters.

The birth of a son, more so than just the birth of a child, is a real "chest puffer." The social pressure to sire a son is so high that it practically discounts the birth of a daughter in our male-preferred society. The expectation for a son is so high that sometimes a man is thought not to be a man until he can say, "That's my boy!" James Brown expressed these dynamics by singing, "This is a man's world; but it wouldn't be nothing—*nothing*—without a woman or a girl." With this ideology as a guide, we continue to insist that the primary measurement of manhood is the siring of sons. And because daughters tend to be less of a measurement for manhood, they are given a secondary place in this male-preferred society. I recall being told by one African American man, "It's good you have a daughter. Daughters will take care of you in your old age."

I had an uncle who had two children. His firstborn was a daughter. His wife reported that he was happy when his daughter was born. His pride as a father was obvious. The special bond that everyone expects to be between a father and his daughter was present. His wife went on to say, however, that when his second child was born—a son—her husband was overjoyed! She received a bouquet of roses and statements of appreciation at the birth of their son that she did not receive after their first child was born. Another father whose firstborn was a girl reported his experience at the delivery of his second child: "When he came out, I shouted, 'Look at those balls!'" This phenomenon is seen time and time again. It is not unusual for a father of daughters to express great joy at the birth of a grandson who becomes the son he never had.

Many a firstborn daughter has been substituted as first in Daddy's heart by the birth of a son who becomes number one. This is a painful reality for many a daughter, and it communicates to boys very early that men are the most important beings in this society. For boys, this not only results in a twisted view of themselves; it also promotes the defensiveness within women that men often despise. Men often accuse women of being too independent and not allowing men to lead. And yet, if fathers reject their daughters out of a preference for sons, daughters must protect themselves against the pain of that past rejection. They must protect themselves against experiencing the painful rejection of another man who is supposed to love them. Having been rejected in the past, many women defend themselves to avoid the pain of rejection in the future. Men regularly blame mothers for the defensiveness they encounter in women, but sometimes that defensiveness is the result of a father's rejection.

The Measure of a Man

Anatomy continues to be the premier mark of manhood. While sirehood becomes the social rite of passage from boyhood to manhood, the size of the male genitalia is an important statement about what it means to be a man. And, of course, the strongest statement to be made publicly is the one a man's bulge makes, in its relaxed state, in his pants. In those instances where a man's endowment must be left to the imagination, the size of his hands and feet become the public representatives of size. Whereas manhood should be measured by the depths of a man's passion for moral uprightness and the content of his character, the standard of measurement for manhood more often comes down to his anatomy and sexual performance. Instead of praising the lengths to which he will go to do the right thing, there tends to be more emphasis placed on the length of his erection and the number of children that result.

The stereotype that purports the enormous size of the Black male genitalia has been ingrained upon the Black male psyche and deeply embedded within American culture. The myths developed around this belief have fueled taboos, accusations, discrimination, and sexualized violence against African American men. Social anxiety has developed around beliefs in Black hypersexuality and intimidating sexual prowess. These "urban legends" have resulted in a range of sexual taboos and descriptions of Black men as sexual predators. The anxiety associated with Black men as being sexually superior and sexually aggressive has resulted in accusations of Black men smoldering for or raping white women. Anxiety related to Black male sexuality has often resulted in strict social codes being instituted to keep Black men away from white women, which sometimes has resulted in employment discrimination. Another historic coping strategy for the anxiety America experienced as a result of Black male sexuality was to mutilate Black men by castration as part of the ritualized practice of lynching. Envy of the Black male genitalia became the coveted prize of the lynch mob.

Although the Black male genitalia stereotype has had many negative consequences for African American men, many Black men have believed themselves to possess the most endowed genitalia on the planet. They have not only taken pride in this stereotype; this stereotype has become a symbol of their manhood. Beyond the shadow of a doubt, to the male mind and ego, SIZE MATTERS! There are more jokes than can be listed that witness to the importance of size. The joke, no matter how it is told, almost always includes a final test: the comparison that proves who is most endowed—small genitalia, small man. For the small man, there is significant locker room embarrassment and never-ending ridicule. The ridicule somehow regularly includes a comment regarding his small size being related to his white genes. The force of the joke is if he were a "real" Black man he would have Black-size genitalia, meaning large—Big genitalia, Big Man. For this man, there is both pride and envy as he walks through the locker room with his towel across his shoulder rather than wrapped around his waist.

Sirehood tends to be the public proof of Black manhood. Through sirehood, a man's anatomical correctness, power, and prowess are considered to be revealed. Even the softest of men is affirmed as a man after the birth of a child. But what of the man and his partner who suffer with infertility? The hidden code within sirehood is the understanding that regardless of a man's genitalia size, a baby is evidence that he has done his job. A baby says, "Manhood confirmed!"

My wife and I suffered with infertility for many years. For years we enlisted medical technology to aid in our desire to have a child. During one of our visits to the fertility clinic we sat uncomfortably in the waiting area. When the nurse came out to let me know that it was my time to supply my specimen, I'm sure she thought she was speaking in an affirming way when she invited me by saying, "Follow me, Sire." I, however, was not affirmed. In fact, I felt more humiliation than had she simply said, "Follow me, please." Again, when manhood is grounded in anatomy and sirehood, the celebration of new life is lost to a focus on sexual performance. Sirehood can actually be very destructive of the strength to love as the essence of manhood. Sirehood is empty and has no witness of divine purpose or sacred intentionality.

King of His Castle

Almost everyone is familiar with the saying "A man's home is his castle." This, of course, is an interesting statement within a culture that does not have castles. Nevertheless, the saying declares that no matter what a man's station or status in life, he is the king of his house; and his home, no matter what size, is his castle. This is a curious thought after discussing the idea that size matters. The saying suggests that a man, as king, is surrounded by the subjects of his authority. As king of his castle, he is the sire, the ruler, the head of his kingdom household. The idea of his home being his castle affirms his sense of sirehood as an individual who stands alone on top. The saying supports the selfishness that the larger society has fostered and encourages.

The idea of king of the castle is not a healthy image for African American men to live into. It is an image that continues to advocate selfishness and the degradation of daughters. The king is socialized to have male heirs. In a male-preferred society, he must be able to pass his rule to a royal prince who will carry on the king's name and inherit the king's possessions. He gains social immortality through his son "begetting" sons. A princess within that system tends not to inherit. Instead, she is married off to form new social and political alliances. Again, within this male-preferred society, we still live beneath strong notions that men take possession of women, and women are given in marriage. It is His Royal Highness that sends forth as well as gives in marriage. It is imperative that we develop alternative understandings of what it means to be Black men in America.

Referring back to a point made in chapter 1, because of the racial oppression that African American men regularly experience, having a place like one's home, where one's voice is not belittled or challenged, is critical. In a world that regards African American men as boys for life, to have a place where we are unquestionably men gives us strength to endure the cruelty imposed by American life. As African American men, we regularly experience social abuse and are misused as we go about our daily routines. Being revered and catered to as sire in the home can have a soothing effect that can help subdue the rage we carry within, which comes from interacting with those who see us as less than human. When we come home we want to feel that no one has authority over us in our own home. This is why proving our manhood to others and to ourselves has historically been so important. The problem is we have often become abusive of others by seeking to overcome the abuses we have experienced.

The link between castle, sirehood, and manhood also clarifies our desire for "sexual healing" as such an important activity at the close of the day. Since sex is the way the man-child copes with rage, being served sex in his castle says he is truly "the man." One man put it this way: "After working with a bunch of racist dudes all day in addition to my body aching from the work, when I get home I want to sit down to a nice meal prepared by my wife. Maybe get a little massage and have her ask me, 'Hey, Babe, how was your day?' Have her give me some nice sex and then go to sleep. I don't need any fussing or arguing." Although the specifics of the statement may vary, the basics of the statement are pretty much the same for many men. Being king of the castle is very connected to a desire many men have to be made to feel like they are "the man." Sirehood is about physical satisfaction—the physical pleasures of food and sex—and social immortality. In order to grow and mature beyond sirehood, our ultimate definition and measurement of manhood must be grounded in features of human beingness other than anatomy and physicality. African American men are generally criminalized based on anatomy and physicality. It only makes sense that we are redeemed by attributes other than the ones that condemn us; and yet, the condemned parts must also be redeemed—hopefully by those same newly identified redeeming attributes.

Fathers Affirming Manhood

We have talked quite a bit about African American sirehood. It is important to recognize the destructive impact that sirehood has on the journey to manhood. Sirehood can stunt the maturation process by causing boys to believe they have matured into men. Sirehood causes boys to assume the title of men without learning, growing into, and accepting the full responsibility of manhood. This is exactly why the harsh criticism many men experience as they irresponsibly go through life is not entirely unfair. Is this another leftover from slavery in America? Without a doubt, sirehood was the norm, and paternal irresponsibility was the design of the slaveholder. But since there was active resistance to the dehumanization of slavery on so many levels, it is vitally important that we reclaim the tradition of African American fatherhood and resist the selfish, immature legacy of sirehood.

Let's now talk more directly about African American fatherhood as a sign of mature manhood and a symbol of community life. If sirehood is selfish, then fatherhood is generous. If sirehood thinks only of how to satisfy the body, then fatherhood thinks constantly of how to enhance the family and community. If sirehood abandons, then fatherhood clings. If sirehood takes, then fatherhood gives. If sirehood boasts about the self, then fatherhood brags about the blessing and giftedness of his children. Fatherhood exists at the positive, opposite extreme of sirehood. As a sign and symbol of manhood, fatherhood is a gift to his family and the larger community.

Sireless Fatherhood

The conversation thus far has focused on and emphasized African American fatherhood. The focus has been on fatherhood essentially because sirehood has been one of the primary markers of Black manhood. As we have discussed, from the moment a boy sires a child, that boy socially, though not necessarily emotionally, makes the transition from boyhood to manhood. Sirehood has largely been our most significant rite of passage from boys into men. Consequently, if we are going to reconstruct our sense of self as men, we must reevaluate the ideas that give meaning to our lives as men. This means we must reinterpret fatherhood to be distinguished from sirehood. We need to shift from what has been the standard measure of manhood to new set of qualifications for manhood. Accordingly, our definition of fatherhood also needs to be expanded.

Fatherhood, like manhood, cannot be dependent upon sirehood. Although men who have not sired a child might consider themselves to be excluded from this conversation, I want to bring forward the African American legacy of men who have been sireless fathers within our community. Certainly, I do not want to exclude any man from the conversation, but I am also not stretching the facts to include all men in the discussion. We have many generations of men—dignified men—who have stood as pillars of the community and have modeled manhood. They pulled boys and young fathers beneath their strong arms and guarded, guided, and provided for their well-being. All boys became the sons of these dignified men of the community. They regularly adopted the boys who were left fatherless by sirehood. Everyone in the community knew them by name and respected them as upright, hardworking, and dedicated men. These men taught the benefits of hard work and self-sacrifice for the good of the community. They were churchmen, spiritual men, men dedicated to the principles of cooperation for survival. This model of manhood embodied by these men was about blood, sweat, and unseen tears as they sought to build a better tomorrow for everyone.

Culturally, the transition from boyhood to manhood has been less about an age distinction and more about a siring activity. Therefore, this siring transition has been less about a paternal responsibility and more about a shift in social stature. Since the dominant message of siring carries a meaning of irresponsibility with it, the true meaning of fatherhood has been a mystery to many young men. With men's culture placing social emphasis upon siring children as the rite of passage to transition from boyhood to manhood, and begetting sons as the measure of manhood, we socially and culturally exclude many brothers from the ranks of manhood. However, because fatherhood at its very core says that as men we have accepted responsibility for our actions, responsibility for the next generation, and responsibility to care for and nurture everyone we encounter in our daily living, a man and fatherhood are measured by the passions of his heart and the strength of his spirit, not by the activity of his loins. It is his heart and soul that give him staying power. Combine staying power with his prowess to save the community from destruction—now that's a real man! This is the lesson that men need to be teaching boys.

Biblical Character Study

To reflect on these dynamics, let us consider the life and times of the great patriarch Abraham. Whenever we think of or identify someone as "great," we are identifying something outstanding about the person's life achievements or character. The great pyramids are not identified as great because they are small and non-distinctive. Their dimensions and stature make them stand out among the pyramids. Likewise, to identify Abraham as great suggests that he had a quality of stature that caused him to tower above ordinary men. And the fact that he was identified as a patriarch says that he was a leader among men. Unfortunately, a close examination of Abraham's life suggests that he was neither a cut above nor a leader among men. The details of his life, especially in relation to his sons, suggest that he did not live up to his reputation as one blessed of God to be a father of many nations. He was really closer to having been a sire of many nations.

Abraham's story is heavy laden with situations that suggest he preferred to be a follower rather than a leader. Without a doubt, everyone cannot be a leader. We do need some people to be followers. Yet Abraham's story suggests that there were many times when he should have stepped forward to function as leader but he chose to hide instead of taking a stand. Although there are many instances in his life in which he might be called irresponsible as a man, husband, and father, I will limit my considerations to his relationship with his children. As the father of many children, he never treated them in ways we believe a loving protective father should treat his children. Time and time again, he sacrificed his relationship with his children by creating distance between his children and himself. Furthermore, instead of cultivating a loving home, Abraham provoked sibling rivalries.

In an act of mistrust, Abraham sired Ishmael with his first wife's maidservant, Hagar. Although we do not know much about the quality of that relationship, we do know that as an expectant father he was not attentive to the prenatal care that Hagar received. We know that Sarah treated Hagar severely enough for Hagar to run away. Abraham's complicity with Sarah's cruelty was his expression that Hagar's condition was her responsibility. Abraham said and did nothing to support her or the child developing in her womb. And after Isaac was born and weaned, Abraham sacrificed Ishmael by sending him and his mother Hagar away to die in the wilderness. He eased his conscience by giving them a little something for the journey, but he was clear that he was sending them to their deaths. There was nothing within him that reflected any responsibility for his son.

Through the retelling of the story, we have tended to make him a more affectionate and concerned father with his son Isaac. But, again, there is not much in the story to reflect a close relationship with Isaac. In fact, our tendency to focus on the question of faithfulness and God's provision redirects our sight from seeing the crisis of relationship between a father and his son. Look at this from Isaac's experience. His father deceived him into believing they would together make a sacrifice to God, sharing a father-son moment; but then Isaac discovered he was Abraham's sacrifice. He was deceived, and his trust was betrayed as the knife was raised over his body tied up on the altar of sacrifice. Do you really think that Isaac lay there peacefully, without tears in his eyes? Do you think he did not beg his father not to kill him, with the promise he would be a good boy from then on? I do not believe Isaac trusted his father to be his protector and guide ever again.

Abraham was going to murder his son Isaac in the name of sacrifice. Did you ever wonder how it was that Abraham could find the strength to tie up his son and raise the knife to kill him? When we look at Abraham's life as a whole, we see it was easy for him, and he did it time and time again. Because he had already sacrificed Ishmael, distancing himself from Isaac in order to sacrifice him was not so difficult. Even in old age, a time when we tend to desire to be surrounded by our children, Abraham once again created distance between himself and his sons. He gave them gifts, perhaps not very different from giving Ishmael a bottle of water, and sent them all away from his sight. His life does not reflect that he ever grew beyond sirehood. Let us not be men who model our lives after Abraham. Let us hold all of our children near to our hearts and never let them go.

CHAPTER THREE

Men and Boys: Mentoring African American Fathers and Sons

We have talked about the movement from boys to men and the image of men to boys. Let's now move our conversation along to another area of concern. Let's talk about the dynamics between men and boys. Considering the multiple attitudes and difficulties I have been reviewing, what lessons are men sharing with boys on a daily basis? The relationships between fathers and sons and men and boys lay the foundation for manhood and frame the core of men's spirituality. Built into this dynamic is the need to learn in a relationship of mutual trust. This also means men and boys must submit to the dynamics of learning. If a man is not able to communicate submission as a statement of respect and not a sign of weakness, then boys learn very quickly that manhood and strength are only and always about physical strength and brutality.

Men must be responsible participants in the lives of sons and boys by teaching them the Ecclesiastical lesson of "a time for everything under heaven" (3:1). We must teach and learn that showing strength physically requires them to be strong spiritually, and showing strength spiritually requires them to be strong physically. Perhaps the best way to share this lesson is to teach *resistance*. Teaching resistance is not teaching boys to be foolishly stubborn. To the contrary, it is teaching boys how to stand for what is right, good, and true about themselves and the world in which we live.

To once again restate: while the focus is on the dynamics between men and boys, these dynamics have a direct effect upon how we view women and girls. If boys are taught to always think of themselves and their desires exclusively when relating to women, then boys are being taught that abusing women and girls is what men are supposed to do. It is absolutely critical that we resist the societal influence that directs us to remain immature boys. This chapter is a review of American society's lesson plan for the development of Black men. It is imperative that African American men take the responsibility for helping boys and men develop into healthy, mature men. The system designed to facilitate the growth process of men and boys is called *mentoring*.

What Is Mentoring?

Mentoring is a teaching-learning relationship grounded in growth and mutual respect. It is a covenantal relationship rooted in trust. The mentor and mentee form a bond of commitment that declares they will face all of life's challenges together. Without this bond of trust, a mentoring relationship will be short-lived. Mentoring is understood to be a supportive relationship that does not have family ties as its foundation. In some instances, it becomes an additional network of support for the family. In other instances, mentoring aids the young man as he seeks to ensure the prosperous future of his growing family.

The mentoring process begins as a mutual selection process. The relationship works best when it is grounded in common interests. Common interests help keep the relationship from becoming frustrating and antagonistic. If the relationship is more frustrating and antagonistic than fulfilling and enjoyable, then it may be better for the two to seek a more fulfilling mentoring relationship. The mentor has to be confident in his manhood and comfortable enough to openly share. He must be able to be vulnerable and self-disclosing with his mentee. Likewise, the mentee must be comfortable enough to openly share with the mentor. It is this open dialogue and engagement in give-and-take that allows for a mentoring relationship to be a healthy and growth-oriented relationship.

Many people think of mentoring as an older person identifying a younger person who can be molded and formed into the older person's image. That understanding of mentoring, however, is closer to a cloning process than it is to mentoring. As I've already stated, the mentoring relationship is based on common interests. It is not based on how much a young person reminds the mentor of himself when he was the mentee's age. To approach mentoring as a process of recreating oneself is abusive. It overlooks the individuality and giftedness of the young person. At the same time, the mentor does further damage by refusing to listen to the young person's voice. A healthy mentoring relationship is grounded, in every way, in the mutual give-and-take of life experiences.

We should not think that we will only encounter one mentor to carry us through our entire lives. As every man grows and develops, life's circumstances will present him with different challenges. No single person is capable of facing every challenge alone. Neither is any single person capable of addressing every possible life experience from the perspective of his own story. Each of us will have experiences that will equip us to share with someone. But everyone will not have the same experiences in life, even as Black men in America. Although everyone has something they can share with someone else, everyone is not equipped to mentor without some preparation. Just being able to recite one's success story is not sufficient for a mentoring relationship. A man must be able to be reflective about the story he tells. He must tell the right story and be able to answer difficult questions about the story that has been told.

For example, I grew up in the suburbs of a small city located in central Pennsylvania. I know how to negotiate small-city life with the suburbs as a home base. I know very little about how to face life's challenges within a large urban center. I have had to learn how to live within an urban metropolitan area. This means, in the course of my professional development, I have had to allow many different persons to educate me (mentor me) on what to do and what not to do when living in an urban metropolitan environment. It is not just navigating living space; there is often a different work ethic that exists between the urban center and the small city.

We all know the importance of learning by doing. The foundation of mentoring, however, is that you are learning by doing with the aid and support of someone who has already walked the path. The mentor is someone who has already completed the task successfully. Although none of us will always have success at everything we do, we know that we can learn from our failures. As a result, the mentor is also someone who does not just share his successes. A mentor must also be able to share his failures along with the steps he took as he attempted to learn from his mistakes. This is the realm of relationship where we are able to see the benefits of openness and mutuality in mentoring.

A mentor is someone who is first and foremost committed to helping another person fulfill his hopes and dreams in life. Identifying a mentee is not the same as identifying a protégé. Again, the mentoring relationship is not about molding someone into one's own image. Mentoring is about guiding someone through difficult times and relationships. It is about celebrating with someone when he has overcome an obstacle. It is about lamenting with someone when the challenge feels too much to bear. It is about grieving with someone over the losses and the failures, while at the same time staying close enough to give the reassurance that all is not lost. It affirms that it is not necessary for the mentee to feel like he has to pick himself up, because there is someone who is present to give a helping hand. The mentor's strong arms of support and encouragement communicate, in spite of the pain, "We are going to get through this together." The mentor reassures to help the mentee overcome any feelings of embarrassment and frustration. The mentor does all this because he desires to see the mentee succeed. There is, however, a delicate balancing act that must be maintained. The mentor does not want to become a crutch for the mentee. As a result, the mentor must always remain conscious of working with—not performing the task for—the mentee.

Just as the mentor must remain conscious of his role in the mentoring relationship, the mentee also has an important part to play. The mentee must be willing to listen to stories. Narrative has been one of the leading teaching tools of African American culture. Moral development and basic life skills have been communicated through storytelling. As we identify with the characters within the stories and think about how the hero of the story has gotten out of different situations, we learn how we are to live life. The listening that is vital today is an intergenerational listening. Unfortunately, there are forces within the culture that discourage intergenerational listening. Hence, the challenge for the mentee is to be able to listen to the mentor's story with openness and a sense of anticipation for what will be learned from the story.

I grew up with the adage "A hard head makes a soft butt." The meaning of that saying emphasizes the importance of listening to statements that can help one avoid difficult and even painful situations. It means listen *and* learn! This is a real challenge for boys and young men. They are supposed to be hard in every way, and nothing should be able to break them down to have any soft spots. *But,* if the mentee is going to benefit from mentoring, he must be open to receiving constructive criticism. Boys and young men are used to being criticized. They tend to hear very harsh and often unfair evaluations of their lives. The type of criticism they are most accustomed to hearing means that many boys and young men are in the habit of silencing intergenerational voices. Many have learned—to the extent that it has become second nature—to ignore the voices of men who could offer sound mentoring through constructive criticism. Constructive criticism is a message that will help the mentee reevaluate his own story and give him the resources to write a new chapter in his life. This also means that mentors must learn to give constructive criticism that promotes growth and to not criticize boys and young men, which will end the relationship.

Mentees must be willing to try new things and invest the energy to try again. Beneath this willingness to try and to invest, there must be a commitment to personal and relational growth. The mentee must be willing to transform the energy of rage, which so often consumes his being, into a creative energy. He must develop a confidence and trust in himself that yields a hope for greater possibilities in life. Rather than yielding to destruction, he focuses on a life of relationships that values everyone around him. In a world that promotes a double standard regarding his being, he must develop a spiritual commitment to life. A spiritual base will give him the resources to resist the overt negativity within the culture and to reach out to others by opposing the individualism that the world encourages him to embrace. His commitment to self and others will reshape life and the community.

Formative Messages

Children are regularly socialized into sex and gender roles through negative reinforcement. As children, we are taught how to live as male and female. We are directed on how to express ourselves in masculine and feminine ways. We are taught that the lines that distinguish the differences between boys and girls are lines that should never be crossed. There are colors deemed appropriate for boys, and those deemed appropriate for girls. We learn very early that the colors represent appropriate behaviors for boys and girls. Children learn that a boy should not act like a girl, and a girl should not act like a boy.

My daughter was watching a Disney feature-length animated movie starring animals. During one of the scenes, a male animal was attacked and began to scream. My daughter, who was seven years old at the time, broke into laughter saying, "He screams like a girl!" This was not an evaluation she learned at home (at least, I hope not!). To the contrary, this was a lesson she learned from the larger society about boys and girls.

These defining and confining messages that teach girls and boys how to be girls and boys permeate our larger culture. The messages are communicated in colors, by clothing, in books, and through games. There are assigned colors for boys and girls, assigned styles of clothing for boys and girls, and assigned activities in books and games for boys and girls. There are toys for girls and toys for boys. If a boy is allowed to play with dolls, the dolls must absolutely be action figures who are quite aggressive. There are thoughts that if boys play "girl games" they will become confused about what it means to be a boy growing into a man. Therefore, there are strict unwritten codes about keeping "girl things" away from boys.

To ensure that one does not behave like the other, behaviors are rewarded and penalized. Unfortunately, penalizing a child to promote particular behaviors is what is emphasized and expressed most often. The early age messages given to boys and girls that instruct them on the ground rules of behavior can actually be quite cruel. What this means is children are beaten, punished, and threatened with disapproval if they do not exhibit the behaviors deemed inappropriate for girls or boys. These punishments tend to be most strongly enacted against boys. In fact, boys are often severely punished for exhibiting behaviors that are thought to represent the feminine. We are all familiar with those punishing attitudes and punitive actions. At playtime, when a boy gets hurt he is encouraged not to feel the hurt, being told, "Big boys don't cry." If he engages in rough play, it is said of him,

"He is *all* boy!" If, however, he expresses emotions or attitudes that are believed to be feminine, he is dealt with roughly in the name of "toughening him up." It is not as though he is unconscious of the differences in treatment between boys and girls. He actually begins to learn from the treatment he receives that boys are favored over girls.

Recognizing the ways boys are punished and even beaten by men when boys do something that is thought to be girlish may help us understand another reason many Black men have such a strong reaction against gay men. Because gayness is thought to be the feminine that has gone unchallenged in a man, men often believe they must beat the gayness out in order to put the man back on track. It is common knowledge that abuse is cyclical—that is, abusers have known some type of abuse in their childhood. Likewise, many men who are aggressively homophobic experienced, either firsthand or by observation, severe punishment as a part of their formation as boys. The overall result is a declaration of there being only one way to be a masculine Black man while simultaneously devaluing the feminine, which can be abused without consequences no matter where it is found. This formation communicates punishment as an attribute of masculinity. The punishment of the perception of femininity within men, and the domination of the feminine within women, is what boys are taught about manhood and masculinity. Because men live beneath the adage "Only the strong survive," it is essential that we develop a new definition of manhood as we continue to talk to one another.

Resistance Culture

When an unjust regime dominates people's lives, there is usually a group identified as the "resistance movement" that opposes the oppressive authorities. The resistance struggles on behalf of the people to restore the dignity that the oppressive authorities deny the people. The resistance struggles to end the tyranny and to restore passion and compassion to daily living. The resistance struggles to encourage the people to live in hope, to live with anticipation, and to live life resisting the evil that surrounds them. By affirming what is good and beautiful in life, the resistance struggles to restore vitality to the people who have been marginalized and downtrodden. Because the tyrannical oppressors distort the lives of the people they deem to be less valuable, life is often marked by abuse and violence. Whereas acts of resistance can be either violent or nonviolent, resistance always requires a commitment of body and spirit.

Resistance is an attribute of African American culture. And creativity, as a vital expression of resistance, is the ground of our being as African Americans. Just as a child is the embodiment of the characteristics and traits of both parents, the child is a new being who is in many ways totally different from each parent. This is a good way of understanding the development of African American culture. It is the offspring of African culture and values and of American culture and values. It is both African and American, and yet it is something new. While it is very American to seek to break the bonds of tyranny, liberty, as a lived reality, is often seen in individual terms. The American idea most notably emphasizes the liberty of the individual. Adjoining African values to American values in resistance efforts means that the work of freedom is a work that focuses on the entire family and the whole community. African American values promote resistance in order to secure liberty and justice for all.

Because of the tyrannical forces that have oppressed African Americans for generations, our work to seek our personhood and freedom has been guided by resistance efforts. We have resisted the dehumanizing definitions of what it means to be Black in America. We have resisted the death-dealing activities that are intended to isolate us. We have resisted the assaults intended to dehumanize us and end our lives. We have resisted in order to survive. We have resisted in order to declare a new way to thrive. We have resisted and refused to accept demoralizing words as defining of our character. We have resisted as our way of celebrating the power of life over death. Resistance is at the center of African American culture and is one of the defining features of Black faith and life. It is my firm belief that if we are going to successfully redefine African American manhood, we must ground ourselves in our cultural inheritance and teach resistance to men and boys.

Teaching Resistance

Teaching resistance needs to become a central component of the mentoring relationship. By teaching resistance we will encourage boys and men to live as integrated, whole, and holy human beings in relationship. Teaching resistance will also direct us to live with our creativity grounded in hope instead of using our creativity as a coping strategy. In other words, instead of displacing our rage and aggression by doing something creative to avoid doing something we will regret, we should intentionally invest in our creative energies to offer a gift to life that is true and good and beautiful.

Think of it this way: birth is creativity at work. Birth is the result of two people who came together and participated in the creative process of bringing forth a new life. However, what two people intend by becoming one body intertwined makes all the difference in the world. Was the coming together the result of lust, which is often displaced aggression? Or was the coming together an expression of love intended to share beauty and celebrate life? Lust is the body's reaction to desire. It is no different than eating to satisfy ravenous hunger. The quality of the food—or even to have an experience with the food—is not a concern. A person just wants to be satisfied. Lust is a disembodied act. Conversely, to act in love is to act with passion and compassion. In terms of our analogy to hunger, love desires to enjoy the experience of eating. It wants to taste and savor every flavor. It is an all-engrossing experience that requires all the senses. Even as you have had your fill of the drink, the cup continues to overflow, stimulating your entire being to want more—and there is more. And in love you are able to talk about the dining experience as you anticipate the next delightful serving in the celebration of sharing this most sacred of experiences. Teaching resistance is to teach embodiment and the strength to love.

Teaching African American men resistance means that we must become more consciously aware of the negative lessons that we have been encouraged to live. Furthermore, it means that we must truly struggle to overcome the rage that has tended to define so much of our being. Teaching resistance means we must first redefine our value system and make life itself our number one priority. But to be as clear as I can on this point, there is no life apart from

Almighty God. So to make life itself our number one priority means that we are acknowledging the Spirit and the presence of God within and all around us. The Spirit is present in every human being. Maintaining this view of life helps us hold God, humanity, and all human activities as central to life. If God is understood to be within and all around, then our core focus becomes a relational focus for daily living. Teaching resistance means we learn to resist all the messages that encourage us to hate one another and to hate ourselves. Teaching resistance means we cease from grounding our masculinity in the activities of abusing femininity. Teaching resistance means we stop focusing on pieces of our bodies. Instead of focusing on a piece, on getting a piece, or on having a piece, we must learn to love and honor the whole body and our entire being—body and soul together.

You Are Not My Father!

Fatherhood, through biology or adoption, is a vital part of African American male identity formation. Although fathers can mentor their sons, mentors can also develop a relationship with boys and young men that can be like the relationship experienced between a father and son. Some of the very best mentoring relationships have an adoptive quality where the mentor identifies the mentee as being "like a son" and the mentee identifies the mentor as being "like a father." Because fathers are so very important to the maturation of boys to men, a father's absence can stunt a boy's growth. Our male-preferred society demands we know our fathers in order to declare who we are and where we come from as men. When a boy is demeaned with the charged "You don't even know who your daddy is!" it is a statement of the fact that fatherhood is an important part of a man's identity. Yes, the statement also carries a demeaning message against the boy's mother, but the greatest impact is the indictment of the father in order to belittle the boy or young man. This is another area of development where teaching resistance becomes meaningful. We must be strong enough to resist the belittling messages that seek to dominate our being.

I was born into a two-parent household. But as can happen with families, marital life deteriorated, and my parents divorced when I was eight. Although I continued to have a relationship with my father, my living with my mother and only visiting with my father meant our relationship was limited. During those early years, the most constant presence of men in my life was my relationship with my grandfathers, uncles, and minister. My father had multiple struggles he was never able to overcome. Consequently, he died when I was fifteen years old. This is often thought to be the age when the father-son relationship is most critical, and mine was completely lost for the rest of my life. Although my father could never be replaced, if it had not been for other men stepping in to fill various aspects of the void with positivity, who knows where I might be today. Without a doubt, my struggles toward manhood were severe, and I did not always negotiate issues well. But had I not had the variety of mentors, positive images of Black manhood, and an affirming family, my positive attributes would not out-weigh my negative.

Whether a boy's father is in the home or not, a mentoring relationship is still important for maturing into manhood. From time to time, being confronted with a boy's anger toward his father is one of the challenges that will be faced while attempting to teach resistance. The anger almost always results from his father's lack of presence in his life. The absence may be the result of sirehood or it may be the result of a father's simple lack of knowledge concerning how to have a father-son growth relationship. The absence may even be the result of the father dying. No matter what the circumstance, when a father is "missing in action" an important growth relationship is missing from the maturation process. Sometimes there is such deep anger and resentment when a boy's biological father is not in his life that he rages against any man who would offer him fatherly advice. In those instances, it is not uncommon to hear, "You are not my father!" When that happens, the mentor must be understanding and must exercise patience in the relationship. Building trust takes time!

Mentoring and the Community

We have identified and discussed the multiple challenges we must face in the mentoring relationship. Extremely important is the fact that both the mentor and the mentee have responsibilities to and for each other in the relationship. We also explored how trust will make or break the mentoring relationship. Teaching resistance has been suggested as the key to positive growth and maturation into manhood. All these dynamics have been explored to identify the importance of mentoring, not only to boys, but also to men. We need one another! This thought can be liberating. It is certainly revolutionary. The acknowledgment that we need one another stands in direct contradiction to the socializing messages that have dominated the maturation process of boys to men. These messages have largely encouraged boys to believe that being a man means one does not need anyone. Learning that no one can live without relationship changes the whole ideal of what it means to live in community.

When a man accepts the responsibilities of full manhood, he will not only support the growth of the next generation of men; he will also support the growth of the larger African American community. By mentoring boys to become responsible adults, we are not only teaching them that they are, in fact, their brothers' keepers. They also become aware of the necessity of being their brothers', sisters', mothers', fathers', and neighbors' keepers as well. This notion of keeping, however, is not the same as the sire who oversees his subject. To the contrary, this alternative notion of keeper means we make a covenant with one another and strive to keep the covenant to do justice, love mercy, walk upright, live with passion, share with compassion, and see the Divine in everything and everyone.

Biblical Character Study

To reflect on these dynamics, let us consider the relationship between Cain and Abel. The story of Cain and Abel is regularly understood by interpreting it as the first murder. And if it is not moralized as the first murder, it is interpreted as a story that shows what happens when jealousy and rage overtake our lives. If we look at the story through these interpretive lenses, however, we miss other important issues that this story communicates. This story is not simply a story of murder; it is a story of fratricide. What could make a man hate his own brother so much that he would kill him? More importantly, what was missing from Cain's life that killing his brother Abel became the answer for his suffering? The answer may be found in the relationship he had with his father.

A close look at the story reveals Adam as an absentee father. The story begins by identifying Adam as the father of Cain and Abel; then Adam is not mentioned again. Perhaps he died. Another possibility is Adam was living the curse of working himself to death. At the very least, there is nothing in the story to suggest that Adam was actively engaged in the lives of his sons. By not being present in the lives and work of Cain and Abel, what did Adam teach his sons? He probably taught them the basics of their jobs. However, it seems that Adam's lack of relationship with his sons resulted in Cain and Abel not having good relational skills. They did not know how to be supportive of each other as brothers. Because Cain did not have a vital father-son relationship with his father, he did not have a clear picture of how to have a relationship with Abel as his younger brother. This very poor father-son dynamic meant it was important for another man to step up to engage Cain's growth needs. Cain and Abel needed mentors. In this instance, God became the mentor.

I stated earlier that the mentoring relationship is a relationship of choice and respect that must be grounded in trust and openness. Cain and Abel both made sacrifices. We know that each sacrificed from his labor and that one was acceptable and one was not. Unfortunately, we do not know why Cain's offering was not acceptable. The common interpretation is that Cain offered the worst of his crop; but that is not what the story says. Instead of having a conversation about what Cain did that was unacceptable, favoritism was shown to Abel without helping Cain improve. In that way, God's words were received as sharp criticism and not reflective engagement on what to do and what not to do. Cain experienced this exchange as a talking at him instead of the development of a father-son or mentor-mentee relationship between God and Cain. The favoritism that was shown to Abel did not allow Cain to learn from his mistake, nor did it help him improve his relational skills. We also do not see Abel reaching out to his brother to help him. Feeling completely abandoned and isolated, Cain directed his rage at the one who was receiving the social privileges.

The turmoil we see in Cain is the turmoil we see in every African American young man whose rage grips him and results in an uncontrollable cycle of violence. Without appropriate systems of support and guidance, young men will be gripped by a blinding rage that seems only to be satisfied by destruction. This can be seen in acts that result in making the external environment a mirror reflection of the turmoil that is felt on the inside. This mirroring action is not unlike stepping into the house of an extremely depressed person. The condition of the house is a direct reflection of the depression a person experiences inside his or her body. In addition to physically bringing down the community, rage seeks to destroy the source of the pain. When the source of the pain is from within, as it was with Cain, a young man in pain may seek to kill anyone he thinks contributes to his problem. Consequently, his rage leads to fratricide too. To Cain's mind, Abel contributed to his pain of rejection, so he slew Abel. Because Abel was Cain's brother by birth, he was also murdering a part of his own being—his flesh and blood.

The question that must be asked is: What did Cain learn from his father, Adam, about manhood and emotions? Cain had such poor control over his emotions that he could not see Abel as his brother or as a friend. With Cain blinded by rage, Abel as his brother disappeared and the man who stood before him was an enemy, someone who was keeping him from achieving his desires. Because rage is the result of years of pressed-down emotions, just how much rejection had Cain experienced that his rage was so deep and explosive?

After Cain murdered Abel, he had another conversation with God. During this conversation, Cain declared having no responsibility for his brother's life. Furthermore, his response to God expressed an unwillingness to take responsibility for his brother's death. As a result, he was judged and marked. Because of his mark, he would suffer everywhere he would go. Although he would not be killed because of his mark, he would be seen as an unforgiven murderer who in a fit of rage killed his brother. In order to avoid being marked, or to transform the mark, we must teach resistance. If we do not teach resistance, Cain's story will continue to be a prominent story among African American men. We must stop killing Abel, our brother, our community, our church, and our future generations.

CHAPTER FOUR

Not My Son: African American Fathers and Their Gay Sons

Horace L. Griffin

Heterosexual Fathers of Gay Sons

Joseph and Joe[1]

Joe and his father Joseph shared a typical Black working-class father-son relationship: few words with even less affection. They did not share a space where they discussed their feelings. They did things together when Joseph was young, but as Joseph grew older they grew more and more distant.

In Joe's early life, when he was in elementary school and middle school, his father would often sigh and with a hint of frustration say to him, "You're such a mama's boy." It became more than his father's way of saying to him that he was different from his brothers. Joe and his father both understood this reference as a cut. It is far from the esteemed "all-boy" reference that many heterosexual boys heard.[2] In a male-preferred society, Joe understood, even at a young age, that it was not good to be "a mama's boy."

A decade and a half later, when Joe confirmed his difference as gay to his father, Joe's father responded with a question: "Are you sure you want to be that way?" Joe responded, "I can be no other way." His father's question hangs in the air—a question voiced by countless Black fathers— as a final attempt to take his son to that comfortable, religiously and socially sanctioned realm of heterosexuality. His question is perhaps more for himself than for Joe. Joseph's truth is virtually like every father's: "Not my son. I don't want him to be that way."

Allen II and Allen III

Allen II and Allen III endured a difficult father-son relationship because of Allen II's strong homophobic reactions to his gay son. Allen II made an impressive rise at a university in Chicago, emerging as one of the university's first African American medical school graduates. An orthopedic surgeon, Allen II acquired the financial means to provide a comfortable home for a wife and three sons in an affluent Chicago neighborhood.

While Allen II's oldest son, Allen III, was in high school, Allen II began making thinly veiled and sometimes obvious accusations about Allen III's homosexuality. Allen II began with a sterile comment: "I don't see you developing any relationships with young women, which you should at this age." Since Allen III's initial lack of response did not satisfy his father's probing, Allen II began questioning Allen III about his male friend: "Why does this guy follow you around like a puppy?" Finally, Allen II wanted Allen III to understand his concern. "What's going on with the two of you?" he asked emphatically. Allen III, frustrated with what had become harassment, angrily stated, "There is nothing going on! He's my best friend." These were his high school years. Despite his budding sexual attraction toward males, he could not admit it to his mother and definitely not to his father.

Early in his college years, Allen III began writing down his erotic feelings for men on the back pages of his class notes. Perhaps curious about his son's college learning and sexual longings, Allen II began reading through the notebook that Allen III accidentally left on the dining room table. In these pages, Allen II found proof of what he had been searching for during the last few years: written evidence of his son's attraction to men.

An enraged Allen II began a tirade by first blaming his wife for causing Allen III's gayness. Then, holding up the notebook, he stormed into Allen III's room, asking, **"Who did this to you?"**[3]

Stories reveal our weaknesses and strengths, our prejudices and insecurities. But stories also have power. They have the power to inform, to heal, and to transform. We are "living human documents" of all these stories.[4] Stories help us build relationships—relationships that are fractured, broken, and need mending. Indeed, the relationships of Black fathers and their gay sons must be bridged, healed, and restored for the health of Black families and their mere survival. We can no longer continue to live with blinders or make claims that suggest that gayness is a "white thing."

The above stories are typical stories of Black fathers and their gay sons. They tell the grim tale of Black fathers' general attitude and behavior toward their gay and bisexual sons. They are often stories filled with pain and shame, distance and disappointment, in a world that still finds it radical for a Black father to show expressions of love toward his son. Even when they are not hostile, as in Joe's case, fathers often find themselves unable to relate to their gay sons or their gay sons' relationships and marriages because of misinformed opinions, church teachings, stereotypes, and lies that we have internalized about gay people and African American life. I write from the place of experience as a gay son of a father whose socialization and church teaching in the 1930s and 1940s left him ill prepared for understanding my love relationship with a man. Let's talk about what we usually avoid. Let's talk about the stories of being fathers, sons, Black, and gay.

Don't Ask; Don't Tell

While gayness is regularly stigmatized and seen as a sickness, Black gay sons of the African diaspora bear society's scourge and—more times than not—their father's shame. They live bruised, as displaced males and despised men so often understood by their fathers as an embarrassment to their families and race. Some sons are beginning to express their pain from being outcasts in families and from being falsely accused of destroying Black communities. With sheer determination, Black gay sons are coming out to their fathers as whole men, refusing to remain hidden in the families' closets of shame and ridicule. Black fathers struggle with this confrontation because they come from worlds—religious and secular—that have rewarded them for opposing their gay sons' right simply to *be*.

After the confrontation is over, many Black gay sons find themselves with fathers unprepared to accept their romantic relationships with men. These sons, desiring their fathers' embrace or a table conversation with them about the men they love, may only find peace in knowing that more gay sons will find the courage to come out to their fathers in the future. While some Black sons, in general, suffer pain from the deprivation of loving fathers, gay sons, in particular, may find that it is too much even to hope for their fathers' embrace. Some gay sons brace themselves and live openly before their fathers. Still fewer come out to their fathers, with most not having fathers present for such an encounter. As we have seen in popular culture, some gay sons hide in heterosexual marriages. And with great pain, other gay sons live in silence.

Since we know that stories have healing power, what happens to these fathers and sons who go on living in silence? How severe are the psychic costs for both father and son living in a "don't ask; don't tell" world? What are the social and religious influences that have created such a horrid reality for thousands of gay sons? The causes for this reality are steeped in the U.S. culture's racist and sexist roots of machoism and the religious and social constructions of homophobia.

Black Machoism

We live in a heterosexual male-preferred society. As a result, it is no surprise that the marginalized Black male would take on a hypermasculine, even sexualized, identity in an effort to assert himself as a powerful man. Although white males generally demonstrate similar thinking and behavior, hypermasculinity has special significance among Black males. Given the historical white males' efforts to dominate, vilify, and emasculate Black men through lynchings, beatings, and the media, Black men adopt a tough and often violent exterior in an attempt to gain their place as men. This machoism is understood as representing strength. Men who fail to exhibit such behavior come to be identified as weak and the opposite of male, as in representing women's behavior. In a sexist society, posturing as a hypermasculine male has meaning for all men.

And while Black machoism's short-term gains may make Black men feel powerful, it is ultimately destructive for their relationships with women, men, and themselves. Hardened personalities, fractured father-son relationships, violence, and incarceration can be linked to Black machoism. In relationships and marriages, many women suffer at the hands of violent heterosexual men. This machoism is the result of male insecurity, which further complicates an already complicated Black father-son relationship. In a Black culture that frowns on male closeness, Black men promote a hard, distant, rough, and tough demeanor with one another in order to be considered men.

The Influence of Sexism

Sexist practices—restricting behavior and activities based on sex and gender—cause further harm to men as well as to women. In a society that devalues female and the feminine, the ill effects of prescribed gender roles run deeper than the hurt feelings of a boy screaming or throwing "like a girl." And while it remains a mystery why many behaviors considered good for girls are condemned when exhibited by boys, Black boys have suffered most from adopting the attitude that they must do the opposite of girls. Until Black boys stop accepting messages that qualities such as caring, sensitivity, closeness, intelligence, industriousness, compassion, mutuality, and nurture are for girls, and that boys must be sports-focused, hardened, and distant, Black men will continue leading in crime, incarceration, unemployment, and failure as productive citizens of society.

Although we live in a male-preferred society, ironically, social conventions allow women to be and do things with other women that are condemned when men attempt the same expressions with other men. Women do not receive ridicule when they spend an inordinate amount of time with one another, touch one another, share intimate space with one another, are affectionate with one another, sleep and dance together, or comment on women's physical attractiveness. Here is a good example of the ironic double standard between men and women on the matter of public affection. Remember when Madonna and Britney Spears kissed at the 2003 MTV awards? Most of their fans approved, with not much more than a peep from a few. Spears even shared in an interview that both her parents liked it. Had that happened between two male celebrities showing affection, social outrage would have ended their careers. If P. Diddy and LL Cool J began an awards show with a sexual kiss, there would have been a different reaction. Viewers generally would have concluded that the men engaged in sensual kissing were gay, and the men would have been ridiculed. However, do you remember whether there were accusations of Madonna or Britney being lesbian?

Homophobia in the Culture

Within African American culture, being considered gay is still a bad thing, especially when it involves men. Allen III's father questioned him about his closeness with his male best friend but in all likelihood would not have questioned the sexuality of his daughter if she had been close to a young woman. Some have tried to point to this emphasis on males as more evidence of a sexist culture valuing males. However, it is small comfort to the millions of men—gay and nongay—suffering from relational restrictions and condemnations.

The discomfort of being close to another male is based in homophobia. Homophobia is the fear, alarm, and negative reaction toward affection and erotic expression between members of the same sex, especially male-male. Homophobia is fear, and fear is the root of prejudice. Boys and men are socialized to be homophobic with each other. Homophobic reactions are especially strong when love and affection between men is observed. From the barbershop to the church, Black men are indoctrinated with a heavy emphasis on being married to women. Nathan McCall, an inmate turned author, wrote a book entitled *Makes Me Wanna Holler*. In his book, McCall describes the ways Black boys receive approval from older Black men when they express a strong attraction to girls. Men generally affirm the view that boys achieve manhood by engaging in sexual intercourse with a female. Although many churches officially disapprove of sex before marriage, churches teach boys very early that they can be men of God only by receiving a woman as Adam received Eve.

America's Changing Scene

Given some of the changes in social expression, it could be said we are living in a post-feminist America. For example, showing emotion is now more acceptable for men. We have, as an American culture, come through the period where men were encouraged to get in touch with their feminine side. As a result, we think nothing of professional athletes hugging and crying. Progressive-minded men are challenging rigid male posturing as unhealthy and silly. Yet there are still many signs that men have a long way to go. Black machoism seems to have remained beyond the reach of a campaign to get in touch with our feminine side. Even as Black men attempt to be closer, our behavior is often at odds with our thinking. This struggle to be close yet distant can be observed in the typical macho hug where a half embrace and a fisted handshake held chest high prevent men from touching chest to chest. The fear of being gay is always lurking somewhere in the background.

In social and religious settings, Black fathers hear comments, jokes, and sermons that tell them their gay sons are bad, flawed, weak abominations—not men. These attitudes are generally not viewed as problems. To the contrary, "real" Black men are expected to hold and espouse these attitudes. In fact, in our heterosexual male-preferred Black community, Black fathers receive little challenge or differing information to effect any change in their hypermasculine, antihomosexual attitudes.

It is essential that we become more directed toward challenging one another regarding this time-honored antihomosexual ideology. Without a doubt, this challenge will be met with resistance from older men and more conservative younger men. Older Black fathers grew up having to defend their manhood in the face of being called "boy." Through the years, we laughed at the negative stereotyping of gay men in the blaxploitation films of the 1970s, Eddie Murphy's homophobic "faggot" jokes, and *In Living Color's* homophobic buffoonery. Another generation of young Black fathers injected themselves with the antigay Black comedians of Comedy Central and the antigay hip-hop and rap lyrics of DMX, Ice Cube, Buju Banton, and Eminem. They all have done a great disservice to gay men. These generations of messages, which have been internalized, have left fathers believing that their gay sons are sick, confused, weak men being laughed at by the fellas with whom they once hung out.

The Stories of Joe and Allen

Joseph found himself working through many feelings about his gay son Joe. Previously, hearing comments about gays had no relation to his life, but now these comments were about his son. "You know they're talking about you," Joseph expressed to Joe, clearly bothered by the homophobia. Joe would shrug away these feelings but recognized the unfairness facing gay men like himself. All his life he had shrugged away comments about his gayness, even the "mama's boy" comments that separated him and made him feel like he was bad. These behaviors reminded Joe, Allen III, and others of the not-too-distant past when whites, through their racist comments and actions, constantly found ways to humiliate Blacks.

Over the past two decades, the misdeeds of racists have been condemned by society at large. Many have questioned why similar attitudes and behaviors against gays are not also condemned. In our social history, Black men were regarded as sexual predators always prowling to rape white women. Similarly, the gay man is seen as a predator who prowls and abuses men and boys. Allen II's question to Allen III—"Who did this to you?"—comes from an indoctrination, that men become gay through some traumatic rape from older, predatory homosexual men. Allen II's rage stirred from notions that gays are sick, weak, disordered, and predatory. He had been socialized to think that as a responsible father, he must straighten out his misguided son, either through therapy or religious intervention.

In most Black homes, the religious intervention would be the option of choice. Because of Allen II's educated class and affluent background, however, he was led to seek therapy for his son in the way upper-middle-class families seek rehabilitation for their drug-addicted or alcoholic adolescent sons or daughters. In 1977, the American Psychological Association defined homosexuality as a mental disorder—a treatable disease. Allen III only agreed with his parents' suggestion for therapy to placate them. He never felt that his gayness resulted from a mental disorder that would change with therapy. For the next twenty years, Allen III expressed that his father never telephoned or visited him. His father never saw where or how he lived. Allen III and his brothers strongly feel that it had to do with their father's fear that Allen III's boyfriend or partner would answer the call or door. Despite his ability to understand the complexity of the world, Allen III's father displayed much fear in entering the different world of his son.

Gay sons generally must help their fathers move beyond such fears if there is to be any substantive relationship. After many years of reaching out to his father, Allen III could see his father softening, trying to love the son whom the world had defined as unworthy of love. On a visit a few years before his father's death, just before he left his father's house Allen III witnessed his father crying. Allen II attempted reconciliation with his son, in perhaps the only way he knew how, by saying, "I just wanted you to be OK." In 1999, Allen II died before so many things could be realized in his relationship with his son. Helping gay sons to "be OK" will not happen by rejection and total isolation. Allen II typifies fathers' difficulties in understanding their sons' gayness. However, there is one group of fathers who understand the intense struggle their sons face—gay and bisexual fathers.

Gay and Bisexual Fathers of Gay Sons

Another reality we need to talk about is gay fathers who also have straight and gay sons. I commented earlier that many gay men made—and continue to make—a decision to hide their gayness in marriage to women and to live closeted lives. In order to receive social, religious, and family sanction, many gay men get married and have children to avoid the persecution and loneliness still facing many gay men. Many still cannot muster the moral courage to be "out" and to live as gay men within their families, churches, communities, and society. However, an increasing number of gay men are living with integrity and are getting married to men and adopting children. Thus, they are out gay fathers with children. There are also bisexual men—men who are sexually attracted to both women and men—who can, and often do, choose to get married to women, sometimes for the same reasons I have already stated. Although not all gay and bisexual men married to women demonstrate acceptance of their gay sons, there does not appear to be the attack on their gay sons that often occurs among many heterosexual fathers of gay sons.

Reverend Davis and James

The Reverend Davis is a gay pastor of a large metropolitan congregation in the South. His son recently came out and, as a result of his son's coming out, Rev. Davis has acknowledged his own gayness. Rev. Davis struggled with his gayness for years as a traditional Baptist pastor. He married James's mother in the mid-1970s and lived a traditional heterosexual life.

Growing up, James had a close relationship with his father. He remembers a caring, compassionate father who was fun-loving and outgoing. Although there were church people frequently around, James states, "Dad always took time to play with us, read stories, take us out to restaurants and movies, and do the normal things with us that fathers do with their kids."

James realized in his teen years that he was gay but found establishing a gay identity in a southern Baptist church difficult. He understands that he was fortunate to have a father who accepted gay people in the church. And though homosexuality was not discussed, he did not grow up hearing homophobic comments or sermons about gays. His father always stressed treating others as you want to be treated. Still, James found it difficult to tell his father that he was gay.

Being a pastor's son, he involved himself in the usual church and youth activities, eventually going into the ministry. After college, James decided that he had to tell his father and mother about his being gay. He had begun to date and felt like he was hiding something from them. When he told his parents, his father demonstrated acceptance and love just as James had imagined. Coming out lifted a huge burden from James and allowed him the freedom to be himself. Rev. Davis had thought that his son was gay when his son was a child but decided that he would wait until James became ready to live as himself. When he told James that he created a safe space for him, James cried tears of joy, realizing that his experience was special and rare.

James encouraged his father to begin a ministry that moved people away from the theology and bigotry against gay people that people had been taught. When examining the Gospels, Rev. Davis did not find it difficult to respond to James's request. He argued that the gospel of Jesus makes it easy to include gays as equal sisters and brothers in the church. It has always been there, but people have chosen to ignore it because it does not satisfy their prejudices against gays. In this climate, Rev. Davis *could understand his son's struggle to love a man in a hostile church and world.*

As James found liberation for himself, Rev. Davis felt that he must also find liberation. He also believed that his wife deserved more sexual energy and passion than he could give her. When he married thirty years ago, he found himself in turmoil over his sexual orientation. He had been led to believe by many sermons, church messages, and conversations with people at the church that he should get married and these feelings would go away. He, like most people in the Black Baptist church, had been taught that homosexuality was a sin, "an abomination in God's sight."

Rev. Davis chose the path of marriage not only because it was acceptable, but also because he believed that by marrying a woman he could be fulfilled. Throughout the marriage he struggled with his sexual passions, eventually realizing that he could only be fulfilled by being with a man. He thought, If heterosexuals can only be fulfilled by being with the opposite gender, then it makes sense that gays can only be fulfilled by being with the same gender. *When his son came out, he and his wife became closer. In this period, he came out to his wife and asked for a divorce, paving the way for a better life for both of them.*

The above story is based on fact but unfortunately does not occur very often. Rev. Davis and James both found peace by living with integrity. James's mother struggled at first but became more comfortable with what had occurred. Though James's family was accepting, he still found it difficult to name himself gay. Unlike heterosexuals, gay sons are weighed down by so many cultural messages that say their very being is wrong. It is difficult to claim a gay identity even when the family environment is not condemning. Gay sons regularly recognize that Black people's having suffered ostracism does not automatically cause them to empathize with the pain others experience.

The Black Church and Homosexuality

The Black church bears a large responsibility for Black people's lack of empathy for gay people. The church's strong influence on Black fathers can be observed throughout Black communities. There is little difference between the antihomosexual message that gays hear in the streets and the message they hear in Black churches. Many times the only difference is that the church message of homosexual hatred is shrouded in God and love. It is rather striking, and sometimes even amusing, to hear Black fathers without any commitment to or active participation in a church reference the Bible on matters of sexuality. You may hear men in barbershops and health clubs reference the Bible in support of their antigay position. What you may never hear from these men, however, is conversation on the Bible's clear prohibition of eating habits, divorce, and adulterous affairs. Obviously, the Bible is regularly being used as justification for their biased views against gay men.

The prominent message about homosexuality that the Black church sends to its members is a negative and judgmental message. For fathers of gay sons, the message feels like it is for them about their sons. The Black church that affirms gays as fully human, created in the image and likeness of God, and that affirms their relationships as blessed and equal to heterosexual relationships, is the exception rather than the rule. When fathers in the Black church consider accepting their gay sons as equal human beings, they find themselves bound by the church's antigay teachings, sermons, and actions advocated by its oftentimes homophobic pastors.

Church Fathers of Gay Sons

It is Sunday morning—any Sunday morning—and Black pastors can be heard across America preaching against gay men. A Black United Methodist pastor in Nashville mimics gay men by swishing before a laughing congregation. A Black Baptist pastor in Washington, DC, declares that homosexuality is "about to destroy the Black community." A Harlem pastor states that homosexuality is against the will of God. A Baptist pastor in Columbia, Missouri, stirs the congregation into a frenzy as he preaches against gays. A Church of God in Christ bishop in Memphis mobilizes his members to discriminate against gay citizens. Considering the widespread homophobic preaching and teaching by Black pastors across the country, it is easy to understand why fathers feel so negatively toward their gay sons. The Black church affirms male-dominated, hypermasculine, homophobic attitudes. Those men who remain in the church emerge as "church fathers" who are resistant to understanding homosexuality and gay people as any-thing other than the presence of immorality in the community. Like agents, they spread the pastors' teachings throughout their fami-lies, workplace, and community. The following case of a Black minister and his gay sons is a poignant example.

Reverend Williams, Michael, and David

The Reverend Williams is a Pentecostal minister in Chicago. He is the father of two gay sons and one heterosexual son. His relationship with his sons is average and pleasant, with minimal engagement about their lives and feelings. For family gatherings, he occasionally visits his older gay son, Michael, at Michael's home. Here he also sees his other gay son, David.

Rev. Williams has been taught by church leaders that homosexuality is sinful, a manifestation of wickedness in the world. He believes that because homosexuality is a sin against God's will, God can deliver people from this sin. Like most fathers and gay sons, they have no conversation about homosexuality other than indirect comments. The Black church and the larger culture have not allowed for helpful conversations about homo-sexuality. Thus, family members find themselves limited to either silence or emotional statements demanding "deliverance" or acceptance. Rev. Williams and his sons have arrived at a truce, a "don't ask; don't tell" practice. Since both sons are single, the gay issue, for the most part, stays in the background like an owl in the night forest.

Rev. Williams says he is praying that God will remove the homosexual demons from his sons. He believes that God delivers people from sin, so he prays that his sons will leave homosexuality in the same manner that a person turns from drug addiction. Since his Pentecostal faith teaches about evil spirits and spiritual warfare, he pities his sons and feels that they are bound by Satan's evil. Rather than seeking to understand his sons' homosexuality as part of their being, just as heterosexuals generally understand their heterosexuality, homosexuality is understood as a bad spirit that needs to be removed.

The older gay son is especially troubled by his father's negative feelings about gay people. Since Michael and David are committed Christians and productive professional people, Michael struggles with the untrue charac-terization of gay people. Michael states, "I think that my father is proud of me and loves me but holds on to this view that something is wrong with

me." David is less vocal about his views but does not like his father's atti-
tude and thinks his father is wrong.

The story of Rev. Williams and his sons is a story shared by thousands of fathers and their gay sons. Black males growing up in the church internalize the "homosexuality as sin" attitude. Few initially differ with this perspective. Church fathers attend Sunday services that reinforce the homophobia they heard as boys. Other resources and responses on the subject rarely appear or appeal to church fathers because of their biblical and church indoctrination. Because the church considers homosexuality a spiritual matter, educational and social-scientific understandings of homosexuality have had little influence. With deep conviction, many Black pastors reinforce the traditional church teachings that say homosexuality is wrong—especially for men. Sometimes the sheer hostility—and even hatred toward gays—boils over in the church as simply pulpit thug talk.

Thug Preaching

A pastor in Washington, DC, preached a castigating message in one of his Sunday sermons. He stated that it took a "real man" to confess Jesus as Lord and Savior, and that "real men" were not "faggots" or "sissies." He then invited all the real men—that is, the straight men—to come forward and praise God that they were not "funny" or "cranky." "Come on down here and walk around and praise God that you are straight," he shouted. "Thank Him that you are straight. All the straight men who are proud to be Christian, who are proud to be men of God, thank God."

Allen III argues that the attack most Black church pastors make on gays and gay relationships by regarding them as sinful is self-serving. In a racist world that continues to deny Black men affirmation and simple respect, Black heterosexual men typically fall into the unfortunate human tendency of raising one group by defining another group as bad and inferior. In this idealized Black heterosexual macho social and religious culture, Black heterosexual men are all too eager for recognition at the expense of their gay brothers. They resist seeing parallels between racism and homophobia, and often use the pulpit before packed church crowds for claiming a superior status over gay men. Sermons like the cruel one mentioned send a message to the heterosexual *and* gay men in the congregation that gays are not "real men."

The preacher of that sermon defines "real men" as men who can confess Jesus as Lord and Savior. Then he makes a leap that is nonsensical. Heterosexual men who confess Jesus are real men, but gay men confessing Jesus as Lord and Savior are not real men. If confessing Jesus as Lord makes one a real man, then why aren't gay men afforded the same status of real men as that of confessing heterosexual men? What does Jesus—not Paul—say about gay men not being real men? Moreover, what does one have to do with the other? If confessing Jesus as Lord makes one a real man, are all those who confess and become saved real men living completely without sin?

After this claim, the pastor invites all the "straight men" to strut before the congregation. In this homophobic and hetero-supremacist moment in worship, no man would want to remain seated. In an effort to preserve their pride, gay men would feel compelled to join this promenade and "testi-lie" in the name of *testify* and give praise. In this kind of world, it is difficult for a gay man to escape feeling shame for not being considered a "real man" and to escape his father's guilt for not having sired one. If a father accepts a position like that of this pastor, how can he celebrate his son's gayness as he would celebrate a son's heterosexuality?

The sermon is curious. Unlike most pastors, this one does not make a theological or biblical link for the unreal gay man. He just takes liberty to denigrate gays—perhaps because he can. Like other homophobic preachers, he knows that he will not receive any challenge from the congregation and will likely become more popular. Since many share his sentiment, even if they disagree with his tactic, fathers will not speak out for their gay sons or many gay sons present will accept one more abuse and excuse the pastor's ignorance. The rest of the heterosexual men will receive a high from another shot of homophobia. And like all people taking toxins into their body, many will not recognize the damage done to their souls and bodies until much later. For the future fathers of gay sons, this day will have done a grave injustice to their father-son relationships.

Love the Sinner; Hate the Sin

In the context of the sermon discussed above, let's revisit Rev. Williams and his sons. Rev. Williams is a product of this orientation—homophobic-God thug talk. Macho pulpit stunts make for harmful father-son relationships, especially in those relationships with bisexual and gay sons. The damage is twofold: (1) my son is not a "real man" and (2) my son cannot love Jesus and is hell bound. In this climate, Rev. Williams can only understand Michael and David as flawed and "outside of the ark of safety." In his attempt to be a good father, he prays to save them from the homosexual demons.

Michael is struggling with feelings of depression about his father's attitude. Michael has been able to accomplish much in a racist *and* homophobic society. He has earned a master's degree as well as numerous professional achievements and awards. By hosting the family gatherings on holidays, he expresses his dedication to his family. Rev. Williams finds himself struggling with Michael and David's erotic love for men. Rev. Williams adopts the position of most church fathers—that is, a "love the sinner and hate the sin" attitude. Although I realize this is a popular teaching to fathers in Black churches, I do not think it is possible to achieve the goal. As I point out in my book *Their Own Receive Them Not: African American Lesbians and Gays in Black Churches*, if same-sex sexual attraction is what makes a person gay, then what is being loved? How can we advocate loving a son's poor immoral choice to have sex with countless numbers of girls, join a gang, live the thug life, or sell illegal drugs, but say we should hate our gay sons? Sexuality is an inextricable part of one's being, like blood type, skin color, and heterosexuality. Therefore, the church position of "love the sinner; hate the sin" has as much success in reality as loving brown-eyed people while hating brown eyes or loving African people while hating what makes them African.

The "love the sinner" position promotes an unhealthy perspective that gay lovemaking and gays themselves are sinful. We need more Christian education regarding the morality of homosexuality and the importance of covenant relationships. This education must include a challenge to Black men for using gays as distractions to cover their own relational hypocrisy.

Those who consider homosexuality to be sinful often understand homosexuality as the worst sin. Black church pastors are generally dedicated to keeping this thinking in place. This thinking often flies in the face of the faith statement that "God sees sin as sin." In the public space of the sermon, gay lovemaking is constructed as sin and described in a way that will achieve a hardy negative response. When a pastor's tone, ridicule, laughter, body language, and misinterpretation of the Scriptures teaches men to think that male tongue-kissing is nasty and disgusting, then disgust is what men will feel.

On a recent Easter Sunday morning, the pastor of a church in Connecticut painted a negative picture of "men tonguing men and women tonguing women." He tapped into years of homophobic indoctrination that gay sexual expressions, especially love between men, are disgusting sexual passions. The congregation responded with shouts, showing their disapproval of homosexuality, as the pastor presented gays as unnatural creatures cursed by God who need Jesus to lift the curse. He constantly justified his rhetoric by stating, "It's in the Bible," a common tactic of homophobic preachers. At that church, the fathers of gay sons received yet another message that their sons were "messed up." One father of a gay son commented that he only had one son and his son turned out like that.

Homosexuality and HIV/AIDS

As mentioned earlier, there is destructive power in this kind of preaching and long-term damage for both the gay son and his father. A lengthy attack on gay sons through a sermon is a throwback to the uncompassionate response of Black pastors during the height of the AIDS crisis in the 1980s and 1990s. No group's response to AIDS could be considered worse than that of Black ministers and the Black church. Guided by fear and misinformation, Black clergy, like white and other clergy, modeled little compassion and much hostility for persons living with AIDS. And although this was not—and is not—a disease that just affected gay men, gay men were disproportionately affected because the first U.S. cases began with gay males.

Despite the reports that challenged the myth that this was God's punishment for homosexuality—for instance, in African countries the majority of people affected were and are heterosexual—Black clergy still seized every opportunity to declare a message that HIV/AIDS was God's scourge on gay people. Black families generally understood AIDS as one more example of God's displeasure with their gay family member's homosexuality. For some fathers of AIDS-infected gay sons, it became easier to express outrage toward their sons than to show compassion and grief for their suffering. For other fathers, it felt like their sons had brought this plague on themselves by disobeying God's will. Those fathers saw the AIDS crisis as a biblical plague that God occasionally rained on people for their wickedness. For those fathers, the condemning message was clear.

Fathers, many taking cues from Black preachers, have shunned their sons, feeling they cannot embrace a diseased child. When hearing about his son's illness in the early 1990s, a Black church father in Alabama refused to let his son come home. The son, a dedicated staff member of a college in Georgia, adopted the college community as family and had his funeral in the college's chapel. Many members of that community still find his banishment by his father unspeakable.

Many Christian gay men struggled with church teachings that said God was indeed punishing them with AIDS for being gay. They felt if they forced themselves to be heterosexual, God would forgive them and give them life. Reggie, who was battling AIDS in the 1990s, was the gay son of a minister. He had listened to his father's homophobia over the years. Throughout most of his thirty-five years, he had been the church pianist at his father's many churches in central Florida. Reggie desperately wanted to be a son of whom his father could be proud.

Despite the fact that Reggie had fought rumors that he was gay, his manner, in so many ways, pointed to his life as a gay man. Still, this did not stop Reggie's efforts of pretending to be heterosexual. He repeatedly denied having AIDS and being gay, even to the point of starting a relationship with a woman. As part of his bargain with God, Reggie decided that a strong denial of homosexuality would win favor with God and give him a second chance at life.

In the late 1990s, I received a full-page newspaper article from Reggie's hometown newspaper. In an unusually long story for a small newspaper, it soon became clear that the article functioned as a message that homosexuals, unlike heterosexuals, end up living destructive lives. The article appeared to be part confession and part sermon by a musician—Reggie. It was an apology to his father (who was dying from cancer), his family, and the church for living a life of "sin." Reggie's description that he "just went bad" and was determined to do his own thing and experience the world as he wanted resulted from a number of things. His pronouncement, however, that this was his choice will be conveniently read by some churches as evidence. They will say, "See, it is a lifestyle choice to live in sin." Reggie described the "lifestyle" of street life, drugs, and so on as being part of a homosexual package. His own self-hatred as a homosexual man and lack of self-awareness was woven together as a decadent life on the fringe.

After describing a wretched life of homelessness, prostitution, and alcoholism, Reggie explained that he hit rock bottom and turned to God for deliverance. He became a minister, was very involved in church, and got engaged to a "wonderful woman." The musician turned minister stated that it was very hard for him to share his testimony at first, particularly about the "homosexual lifestyle" that he lived for awhile. He did not believe that homosexuality was something people were born with. He said, in his case at least, it was a choice. He wrote, "I chose to go into that lifestyle and now I've come out of it." These are the words that church fathers love to hear as they resist the notion that same-sex lovemaking and relationships could be equally satisfying, moral, and as life-giving as many heterosexual relationships. Reggie's story is the story many love to tell: a tragic man hits rock bottom because of his homosexual lifestyle, finds God and a woman, and lives happily ever after.

Unfortunately, Reggie's story does not end like so many wish that it had. Two years later, Reggie died. There are many points in Reggie's story to consider. First, Reggie was typical of many African American gay men who never accept their homosexuality as a good and normal sexual attraction and expression, and later contract AIDS. Like Reggie, the coincidence that AIDS became prevalent among gay men in this country led them to make the false correlation that gay men were being punished for their sin of homosexuality. Furthermore, Reggie had no one to turn to for help in accepting his homosexuality. Not only did he struggle with the shunning by his father and the hatred that he experienced from others in his early life, but as a result of that experience, he internalized those feeling about himself and lived an obnoxious life, guided by self-destructive behaviors, creating a self-fulfilling prophecy for his life to end tragically. Having spent his early life in churches that condemned his homosexuality, Reggie never overcame the teaching that said because he was homosexual he was without value, and he therefore placed himself in situations that would destroy his life. In the end, Reggie never got over his disapproving father.

Reggie's faith became misguided in his quest to find peace with his father and himself. He believed that he would no longer be gay if he developed a relationship with a woman. And he believed he would be cured of his AIDS if he developed a relationship with a woman. In order to "get back into the good graces" of his father and his God, Reggie believed he could use a woman to salvage his relationship with his father and to save his own life. Of course, neither came true. One of the most important messages for Black churches is that one's sexual orientation does not define one's moral character. Just as Reggie described his messed-up life of substance and sexual abuse as a gay man, there are countless heterosexuals abusing drugs, sex, and alcohol in the very same ways.

The negative messages of shame and guilt, religious and social condemnation, and the general lack of affirmation Black gays receive in their families and churches are often the primary causes of their misery, pathology, and sinful behavior—not the homosexual attraction and expression itself. The toxic messages of religious leaders must be challenged and corrected because they contribute to the tragedy and death of gays who are victimized by life and kept from receiving the love and nurture they deserve from their fathers.

In addition to the shame that many gay sons internalize because of the isolation and messages that they receive from their fathers, many deny their homosexuality to win acceptance from their fathers and others. Gay sons with AIDS generally fear family problems and outright rejection once their fathers and family members discover the truth. Since many fear that family members would not welcome their return home, many stay away from home until they can no longer care for themselves. Few expect that their fathers would be there for them.

In cases where fathers were present in the household, mothers often nurtured the relationships with their sons. Black sons struggle with their fathers' absence and long for a parental relationship that could be more empathetic to their struggles as Black men living in a racist society. Others remain hopeful that the church fathers and church leaders will change their attitudes and see gays as children of God in loving, same-gendered relationships blessed by God.

"What Would Jesus Do?" A Pastoral Response

A few years ago, the slogan "What would Jesus do?" became popular, especially in evangelical churches. Many teens donned trendy WWJD bracelets as a reminder to respond as Jesus would respond in various situations. As happens with people who use the Bible in selective ways, the question also found its way into conversations about moral judgment in selective ways. There is a noticeable absence of WWJD regarding homosexuality. It should make a difference to church fathers that Jesus is silent on homosexuality. His silence on homosexuality in all four Gospels ought to make African American fathers think twice before assuming that homosexuality is the great sin that the majority of Black churches declare it to be. If homosexuality were a great sin—or a sin at all—it is reasonable to assume that at some point during his ministry Jesus certainly would have addressed this terrible way of life, as he did other sins. But he did not.

The Gospels are clear about what Jesus would do. We know Jesus *would not* stand outside the church as grieving families screamed with anguish and condemnation that their gay son died in his sins and went to hell. Jesus *would not* be preaching sermons against an entire group of gay people. Jesus *would not* advocate for religious and legal discrimination against gays in the name of being faithful. Ironically, the people Jesus spoke against were people like bigoted pastors, Pharisees, and Sadducees—those engaged in castigating others. He found such self-righteous, rigid approaches antithetical to the gospel he proclaimed.

Jesus preached a clear message of inclusion and demanded that followers treat others as they wished to be treated themselves. Throughout his ministry, he proclaimed liberation for the poor and oppressed. In the same manner that African American preachers have identified Jesus with us in our struggles and oppression, Jesus also sides with gay people in their present struggles and oppression.

Black church fathers and leaders actually rely on Paul for their antihomosexual position. There is a striking irony that some church fathers and leaders are so uncritical of Paul's writing about homosexual activity but have rightfully maintained a critical attitude and sometimes an outright rejection of Paul's injunctions on slavery. It is strange that we who are followers of Jesus rely on Paul's interpretive response to homosexual activity instead of relying on Jesus' noncondemnation of homosexuality. Furthermore, Paul did not speak particularly affirmingly of marriage either.

Like others, I have argued that the Bible is not addressing homosexuality and a gay presence as we interpret the texts in this twenty-first century. I believe that if Paul had been able to observe loving sexual relationships between women and men, and had experienced the witness of gay Christians in churches and communities, and had written about gay people in this context, he would have celebrated gays as God's people. Like Paul, I believe that most Black fathers would do the same if given the opportunity to be in dialogue and relationship with gay family members, friends, and colleagues. When they move beyond their walls of fear, Black fathers will discover the many things they have in common with their gay sons. I firmly believe that Black men—like all men—have the capacity to love and nurture their sons, teach them respect for all human beings, and value their gay sons no less than their heterosexual ones.

Fathers and sons can begin the process of healing by listening to each other share what they want most in life. Conversations can happen in places where men do what they do. Stories can be shared in parks, in restaurants, on fishing boats on a lake, in empty sports fields, or in a favorite room in the house. In a good environment, there is greater potential for calm and openness to new ideas. Of course, spending time is vitally important for improving father-son relationships. When fathers and sons play together, worship together in an affirming environment, travel together, or just watch movies or television together, they will begin experiencing more laughter and joy that will bring them closer together. While it will take time for mending strained or fractured relationships, such gestures will begin the healing process. Later, fathers and sons may begin moving beyond some of the internalized church and social prejudices about gays by reading church materials that accurately inform men about gay Christian relationships.

A number of younger Black men within and outside the church are beginning to challenge the common biblical defense of homophobia. These young fathers argue that the Word has been construed to support a long-held bias against gays rather than becoming a blueprint for Christian living. They argue that there is no justification for emphasizing an expression that is hardly mentioned in the Word while often ignoring those that are mentioned—namely, releasing wealth, prohibitions against divorce, and adultery. Through education, they are realizing that for both their sons and themselves they must move beyond the hate they have internalized.

Indeed, stories can transform us into better human beings. The painful stories of fathers and their gay sons speak to us now. It is up to us to hear these stories and ask ourselves how we should respond. Our acceptance and celebration of gay men offer hope for better relations within families and the household of God. They point us to the beauty of God's diverse creation. When we allow ourselves to appreciate all relationships, to affirm the erotic in all of us, we will proclaim liberation for Black fathers and sons and Black families, and in so doing we will honor God.

PART II

Lessons from Sons Who Father Daughters

CHAPTER FIVE

It's a... Girl: Challenges to African American Manhood and the Birth of a Daughter

Edward P. Wimberly

Let's talk about what happens to our opinions of our manhood when we father daughters and not sons. Our male-preferred society has established the scale that measures manhood with the birth of sons. We are socialized to believe we will only live on if we have a son to carry on our name. We live in fear that our bloodline and family name will end unless we have sons to make us immortal.

Consider the scene. There he stands, poised to burst with pride, awaiting the arrival of his child. He has been waiting to announce to everyone within earshot, "It's a BOY!" There he stands, watching the appearance of head, shoulders, arms, and so on. He begins to speak with great enthusiasm, "It's a..." Then the baby's whole body is revealed, and the enthusiasm wanes. With deep disappointment he breathes, "It's a girl." Perhaps he recovers; perhaps he doesn't. If he does not recover from this emotional loss, he will forsake his responsibility and abandon his daughter. By abandoning her, he loses his own soul. Living with a feeling of abandonment affects our ability to share loving relationships. This chapter explores traditional gender-role expectations and offers an image of father-daughter relationships that promotes affirmation rather than subservience. So let's talk about our responsibility as fathers of daughters.

On Learning to Be a Father

My wife and I have no biological children. I have, however, taken on the responsibilities of fatherhood in many family and nonfamily relationships. This has very much been the case with my three nieces. My brother died in 1996. At that time, two of his daughters were in college and well on their way to adulthood. The youngest girl was nine when her father died. Not having my own birth children meant that my ideas of being a father were largely the result of observation. And, oddly enough, my father did not lay the foundation. I learned about parenting from what I saw in my mother when I was a child. My sister was two years younger than I. My thoughts for what it meant to raise a daughter came from what I saw in my sister as we were growing up in my parents' household.

Although I learned from my mother about the day-to-day activities of fathering daughters, I learned how men should treat women by the way my father supported my mother. My father, who was present in our home, seemed to value my mother's professional identity and throughout their working years supported her effort to be a schoolteacher. He was a pastor in The United Methodist Church. He often sacrificed advancement in the church in order to make sure that my mother's job was not jeopardized by his moving to larger churches. Moreover, *both* my parents were committed to my sister's growth and development in her personal and professional gifts. In short, my father was able to respond to my mother's professional identity and need to have a profession of her own, and he was a relational presence for her. He also was able to respond to the developmental needs of my sister as well. I brought into the relationship with my wife an expectation that I would need to support my wife's professional growth needs as well as her personal growth needs. I also brought with me the expectation that I needed to support any child's growth needs. This was especially true as it related to the growth needs of girls. I learned from my parents the importance of supporting a girl's (as well as a woman's) self-understanding without imposing my own agenda on her.

Concerning my nieces, I have made sure to establish a positive relationship with them. I also have waited for them to bring their concrete expectations to me. My youngest niece, who is now a young adult, initiated opportunities to engage in play with me while she was a preschool child. I seem to have a gift of playfulness. This was confirmed when we lived as a three-generational household raising a surrogate niece when she was between two and five years of age. As my youngest niece began elementary school, she did not need me to play with her. She needed my quiet assurance that I affirmed her whenever she was in my presence. She enjoyed accompanying her twin brother and me to Atlanta Falcons football games.

Another of my brother's adult daughters sought my emotional support when she was preparing for marriage. She expected me to participate in her wedding, as her father would have. Her expectations of my fatherly presence did not end with the nuptials. She expected me to be present when she and her husband celebrated the births and birthdays of their children. She expected me to perform all the roles that my brother would have had he been alive. The oldest niece, who also attends the same church that my wife and I do, experienced the same loving support as her sisters. We enjoy supporting her interests and her professional and marital aspirations as well. Although I have been supportive of all my nieces' professional aspirations, I have lived with the hope that one of my nieces will become a minister.

This chapter will attempt to rectify racism's perversion of Black masculinity. This effort to rectify the damage done to the family will result in a new image of African American manhood. So, let's talk about the importance of changing the image of African American manhood and changing men's role expectations with their daughters.

The Role of Provider

Always in the parenting background of African American fathers and mothers are role expectations. We tend to live with traditional role expectations of a father as provider and a mother as nurturer. Although traditional role expectations continue to be experienced, the traditions have sometimes been modified to not require mothers and wives to be subservient and submissive to fathers and husbands. The removal of the expectation for women to be subservient and submissive within the home is a vitally important shift that needs to be made. We need to advocate rearing daughters who have positive self-esteem, who feel like worthwhile human beings, and who are not subservient to men.[1] Although men have implicit or explicit desires to have sons to carry on the family legacy, these expectations of fatherhood are put in the background when men attempt to respond to the real developmental needs of their daughters. Fathers who take seriously their daughters' growth and maturation help girls value themselves. They encourage their daughters to make contributions to the home and society.

"Indeed, we need to better understand why the notion of the male as provider for his family is so important for both Black men and Black women."[2] This quotation is a concluding thought after a series of in-depth interviews of fifteen African American men and nineteen African American women on questions regarding the roles of Black women and Black men in the home. Not surprising, men and women both expect men to be providers for their families. Also not surprising, a man's self-worth tends to be rooted in his role as provider. This has been our long social history even as both men and women expect women to be nurturers within their family. What may be surprising is that women in African American middle-class families are not expected to be submissive.[3] This study suggests that we can live differently from the ways stereotypes have styled our lives.

Fathers as Providers

Although we live in a male-preferred society, African American families have not been able to survive with a family structure of the "stay-at-home mom." African American women and mothers have had to be active participants in the work of ensuring the financial survival of the family. While the American ideal has been the provider father and the nurturing, stay-at-home mother, African American history has shown social realities that have made it difficult for African American men to be the sole providers. African American men, therefore, are more likely to support their spouses working, given the need for the family to survive. The gender-role distinctions between the provider and domestic tasks within the African American home are not as rigidly defined as tends to be the case in European American families. Although African American women perform the bulk of the domestic work and childcare within the home, more African American men are participating in sharing the load.

African American men are under a lot of pressure to be providers in families, for a variety of reasons. Living into the curse of Adam, we tend to be directed to work ourselves to death as we struggle to be providers. Being a provider is seen as the primary mark of manhood. We seek higher incomes, and sometimes multiple jobs, in an effort to provide for the financial needs of the family. In addition, our wives also expect us to have adequate income for there to be marital happiness and success.

The expectation of African American men and women to play gender-specific roles when it comes to household activities and responsibilities creates very real pressure for both men and women. This is the case for young and old alike. Both men and women define masculinity and femininity in terms of role expectation. Masculinity is defined instrumentally: being a father, husband, and coprovider is necessary for there to be a successful family life. The father as provider can have some nurturing characteristics, and I believe fathers need to assume more nurturing responsibilities—especially as we relate to our daughters.

Traditional models of family life hold that mothers interact more with children, while fathers are disciplinarians. Moreover, because children tend to learn about adulthood and parenting from their fathers and mothers, we tend to pass gender-specific roles on to our children. Most men feel that daughters need their mothers to be strong, nurturing figures. Fathers can be nurturing figures for daughters, but we usually feel there is no substitute for what mothers provide. This view we must change in order to participate more fully in the nurturance of our daughters. Our manhood being so connected to the birth of sons also means we believe boys and girls are different and should be raised differently. We must unhitch our ideas of manhood from the birth of our children. Furthermore, our ideas of raising girls and boys differently often go directly to our beliefs about what boys do to girls. Instead of teaching boys to be respectful, we teach them to be aggressive toward and disrespectful of girls. In the end, we encourage boys to do exactly what we fear they will do to our daughters, which is another reason we prefer sons. While African American fathers prefer specific gender-related tasks in rearing daughters, the key question that needs to be answered is: how should African American fathers relate to their daughters within our male-preferred society?

Suggestions for Change

In addition to my experience of raising my nieces, I have had significant experience as a pastoral counselor working with Black fathers. Here, I will share a counseling relationship to talk about what African American fathers raising daughters brought to the relationship with their daughters. This case, along with some insights provided by one of my African American pastoral counseling colleagues, will be the source of reflections in this section.

The specific case involves a father whose wife ran off with another man, leaving the father to raise a preadolescent teenage daughter. The father was devastated by the loss of his wife. His beliefs about the necessity of raising daughters differently led him to feel he needed some support in raising his daughter. The daughter was unusual in the sense that she had great insight into the needs of her mother, and she accepted the fact that her mother could not be what she as a preadolescent needed in her life. She actually stated that her mother had some unresolved adolescent issues, which her mother needed to address. What this very astute daughter needed, however, was for her father to be a stable presence in her life.

The father was very proud of his daughter's adult qualities, particularly her intelligence and insight about her mother's needs. He appreciated his daughter's adult qualities. Unfortunately, she developed those qualities as a result of reversing roles with her mother. In many ways, the child was the mother of her mother. Although the father liked these adult qualities in his daughter, she was not having her own growth needs met. The father found it easier to relate to her as an adult instead of as his daughter with age-appropriate needs. The growth needs of a preadolescent girl had been completely ignored. An important part of her childhood was being ignored. As a result, the father had difficulty when his daughter was a typical preadolescent who was like her preadolescent peers. The daughter needed her father to relate to her in age-appropriate ways. In short, the father needed to become the nurturing and caring parent struggling with a daughter whose childhood had been denied. He needed support in trying to pull this off without the help of his wife. His daughter's age and social relationships were pulling her into the preadolescent childhood she had lost by mothering an inadequate mother.

What I learned from working with this family is that most men have the capacity to develop relational empathy for their daughters. In this situation, the father's capacity emerged as he was able to listen to his daughter speak about what she was going through in life. My work with this father and daughter focused on helping him develop empathic listening as she spoke of her life. Our listening together enabled both the father and me to understand his daughter's age-appropriate struggles as well as give her gentle guidance as she attempted to live appropriately with her peers and with her father.

As I reflected back on this case, I found the unpublished work of Bernard Kynes very helpful. He wrote a paper entitled "African American Fathers as Caregivers."[4] His basic conclusion is that African American fathers need to be more than just material and instrumental providers for their children. He says that they need to be spiritually, physically, and emotionally accessible to their children. His understanding of accessibility is critical. He emphasizes nurture to describe what he means by accessibility. For him, nurture is what mothers traditionally do for their children; but he also ascribes this characteristic as something that fathers are able to do as well. Nurture, which means to nourish or suckle, to educate, and to foster development, is what we do as parents when we engage in the training and upbringing of children. For Kynes, nurturing is a deeply emotional process, and he knows that African American fathers have the capacity to nurture their children despite popular opinions to the contrary.

Being a nurturer does not mean being soft or weak. The issue that works against African American men being nurturers is "compulsive masculinity [that] refers to males adopting norms of toughness, emotional detachment, sexual conquest, manipulation, and thrill seeking as a response to economic marginality and racial discrimination."[5] Bethany L. Letiecq and Sally A. Koblinsky point out that African American fathers of preschoolers use protective monitoring and nurturing strategies to teach their children about safety and how to protect themselves in violent neighborhoods.[6] Contrary to popular belief, young black fathers tend to be no different from other young fathers in the support they provide to their children.

Furthermore, absentee African American fatherhood is no longer as prevalent as it once was.[7]

The question before us is not whether African American fathers can love their daughters. The question is: Will African American fathers love their daughters enough to nurture them into being all God intends for them to become? The love that is required goes beyond just providing the material needs for growth. There must also be a nurturing emotional connection. The practice of hugging and embracing, not only of infants but also of children throughout the life cycle, communicates heartfelt warmth and acceptance of the child's worth and value as a human being. Nurturing actions like hugging should become routine without becoming empty. Nurturing should be so much a part of our daily lives that our daughters should never have to ask, "What did I do to deserve a hug?" Genuine hugging communicates a profound respect for a person as one who is created in the image of God, and who has been born to carry out a unique calling in life. This unique calling is linked to God's call to participate in God's work that is being carried out on earth.

We should not underestimate the powerful effect acts of love from a father can have on his daughter. A father's physical presence and active engagement in the life of his daughter allows aspects of her father's personality and attitudes to become her own. Through this process of internalization of the father's qualities, the daughter develops an enduring inner source of self-love, which can nourish her whole life. Kynes says:

> Children yearn for their father's physical presence. Children starve for their father's spiritual and emotional presence more. This is to say from the time of birth, children want their fathers to be in the delivery rooms to hold them as well. While in their mother's womb, the child wants the father to be available and accessible. As the child grows through each developmental phase, he or she needs the spirituality, love, grace, guidance, stability, creativity, experience, wisdom, vision, tenderness, firmness, empathy, compassion, moral leadership, and positive attitude from their biological, adoptive, or surrogate father in the flesh.[8]

If we listen carefully, we will hear daughters of all ages speak the need for the physical presence of fathers in their lives, whether fathers live in the home or not. Girls and young women alike point out that facing life without their fathers, who should have been present in their lives, caused them to struggle to develop a sense of love worthiness. Daughters develop their ideals of what they should look for in a life partner from the relationship they have with their fathers. Moreover, fathers often instill in their daughters a sense of what it is like to be a "lady." These dynamics have led many to conclude that young girls who have grown up without the influence of a father often offer sex in exchange for a hope that they might be loved. Fathers need to accept responsibility for the nurture of their daughters because fathers are as important as mothers in rearing daughters. In a society that tends only to promote fathers as providers, we men need to work hard to counter the trend of devaluing the role of fathers as parents.

Living beyond the Disappointment of Not Having Sons

The social structure of American life as a male-preferred society means it is only natural that African American fathers might be disappointed at the birth of a daughter instead of a son. But daughters *are* born, and without them we will not have future generations. We should not take this to say, however, that a woman's only purpose is to give birth to children. This belief is what has distorted the image of womanhood as being less than the image of God. The biblical record is clear on this matter: God created human beings, male *and* female, in the image and likeness of God. As a result, it is imperative that fathers learn to transcend their disappointment and become nurturing, present fathers of daughters. We have the responsibility and therefore must be responsible to love and guide our daughters, even as we would our sons. As your child, a daughter is as much "you" as your son would be.

One place to begin improving the relationship with your daughter is to become a better partner or husband. Because American culture continues to emphasize relationship for girls, your daughter will learn as much about relationships from observing your relationships as she will from being in relationship with you as her father. The dynamics you live before your daughter and with your daughter will form her expectations for the rest of her life. James Brown sang the song "Papa Don't Take No Mess." If you nurture your daughter to live as a strong, secure woman, she will govern her life singing, "Papa don't take no mess, and neither do I!"

Expectant fathers develop ideas about their child who is growing in the womb. Coupled with the hope of a man needing to sire a son is the exaggerated image of Black manhood that has been informed by racism in the United States. As long as we live according to the distorted images of racism, we will continue to be victims of our social history and victimizers of our daughters.

CHAPTER SIX

Daddy's Little Girl: African American Fathers Protecting Their Daughters

Homer U. Ashby Jr.

Sometimes no more than two or three sentences passed between us during the whole time we were together in the office. But I remember those evenings, particularly in the springtime, as very special and satisfying times. —Audre Lorde

The relationship between Black fathers and Black daughters is a special one. Through the work of Black female authors who write about the painful consequences of their Black fathers' absence in their lives, we know the tremendous impact Black fathers have on their Black daughters.[1] Yet father absence and the pain it brings to Black girls is not the only way we know of the specialness of the Black father–Black daughter relationship. In addition to the quotation by Audre Lorde that begins this essay, there is an emotionally moving collection of father-daughter recollections edited by Gloria Wade-Gayles that includes a number of praise songs by Black women to their Black fathers.[2] Because of the vulnerable status of African American males, much more attention has been given to the Black father–Black son relationship. Major conferences such as the Morehouse conference on Black males, held in 1999,[3] highlighted the plight of African American males and the detrimental effects of father absence on their lives. The writings of John Wideman and the anthology created by Houston Baker bear witness to a long-standing interest in the Black father–Black son relationship.[4] Yet as Jonetta Barras notes, there has been much less written about the Black father–Black daughter relationship.

> In 1996, I began reading tons of material and calling experts, including psychologists and sociologists. There were more than two dozen books on the topic of fathers and sons in print that year. Less than a dozen books explored the father-daughter relationship; most of them had been published in the 1980s. Even more important, of the books on fatherless women, none was written by an African American.[5]

Far too much of the emphasis on the relationship between Black children and their parents has been on father absence or single-mother parenthood. This is somewhat understandable because, as the data shows, 57 percent of all Black children grow up in households with a single parent. One-fourth of all Black children grow up in households where the father is absent. Focusing on the absent Black father fits with the demographics. However, without some attention given to the ways in which father presence contributes to the well-being of Black girls, Black sons who wish to be effective Black fathers may not receive the guidance and encouragement they need. This chapter, then, is a Black father's reflection on his relationship with his Black daughter, written for my "sons" who will be raising the next generation of African American women.

The Tremendous Impact of Black Father Absence on Black Daughters

The impact of Black father absence on Black daughters cannot be underestimated. When Black fathers are not present for their daughters, the list of detrimental consequences is staggering. In addition, the impact is so monumental that it has the potential to damage the core of the individual self as well as contribute to a historical thread of enmity between Black men and Black women. For the individual Black woman abandoned by her father, there is susceptibility to what Barras calls the Fatherless Woman Syndrome.

> The key components of the syndrome are rooted in the feeling of being fundamentally unworthy and unlovable. Like a spiral stair-

case without landings, these feelings wind about and lead to chronic rage, anger, and depression that are rooted in our fear of abandonment, rejection, or commitment.[6]

With the Fatherless Woman Syndrome, fatherless women conclude that the absence of their fathers must have had something to do with them. They surmise that perhaps it was their physical features: too dark, too light, too tall, too short, too skinny, or too fat. Perhaps it was something about their personality: too sassy, too insecure, too needy, or too independent. The father's absence was not caused by anything the daughter did or did not do. Yet at a young age daughters put the blame on themselves for their fathers' absence. The daughter conjectures that her father left because of something about her. According to Barras, this results in feelings of guilt, shame, and self-hatred that lead to a fundamental sense of being unworthy and unlovable. The ancillary feelings of rage and anger are directed outward and inward. For those who remain in the daughter's presence, there is rage and anger for whatever they may have contributed to her father's departure. There is rage and anger at herself for whatever contribution she believes she made to her father's departure.

> Initially, I thought to blame my mother for Noel's departure. But then I realized that if I assaulted her, I jeopardized the little love I had. What would happen, I asked myself, if I screamed at her, told her she was the reason he went away? I worried that she might also leave, never to be heard from again. And then, there would be no one there to love me. So, I attacked myself: He left because my skin was too dark, my nose too wide, my hair never stayed down when it was told. Even the space between my teeth was too offensive; years later, my mother suggests we close it. I am the Black sheep no one loves.[7]

And competing with the desperate desire for her father's presence is anger at her father because he deserted her. The daughter feels at a deep level the depression associated with the incredible sense of loss.

> After he left, and I realized he wasn't coming back, I frequently made my way inside the confessional at Epiphany, later at St. Gabriel, sometimes at St. Paul. I fell on the wooden floor rest, my

bony knees whining from the discomfort. "Bless me, Father, for I have sinned," I whispered as the priest positioned his ear close to the mesh opening, listening for me to begin my inventory of offenses. With the sincerity expressed only by the very young, I muttered that I lied when I said I didn't care that Noel was gone. I lied when I said I was happy. I did not know what happiness was.

There was an internal civil war under way; I was too young to explain the battle to anyone, least of all the priest, who engendered reverence. I wanted God to resurrect me, the way he did Jesus Christ. The term *suicide* was foreign to me then. Now, however, I realize that is the word I would have used in the confessional.[8]

The impact remains through adulthood. Barras names these negative impacts as a set of factors. There is the "un" factor: feeling unworthy and unlovable. There is the "triple fears" factor: fear of rejection, fear of abandonment, and fear of commitment. The "sexual healing" factor can lead to behaviors that range from promiscuity to aversion to intimacy. Often having a baby is used as a defense against loneliness. The "over" factor refers to overcompensation (doing too much), overachieving (proving one's self worthy), and oversaturation (consuming too much to make up for the loss). Finally the "rad" factor of **r**age, **a**nger, and **d**epression represents the primary affective responses the fatherless daughter uses to ward off the feelings of loss. The impact of the sense of loss takes many forms: physical, emotional, and spiritual.

Father, what prayer should I say so God might forgive my ugliness and send Noel back? There was no answer, only a prescription for forgiveness. I raced back to the pew, knelt, and recited the prayers, eagerly, eating each word as if it were red, juicy watermelon. I knew when I finished, when I had recited the requisite Our Fathers and Hail Marys, Noel would return. But he didn't come back that day, nor the next. I cried.

I continued to cry for three decades.... Noel had deserted me. He had made me feel loved; he had made me feel wanted. He was the father from whose departure I would never recover. He was gone. Adding to the injury, God had turned his back on me.[9]

The Empowering Impact of Black Father Presence on Black Daughters

Over against the staggering negative impact of Black father absence, there is evidence of the positive, empowering impact Black father presence can have for Black daughters. The word *empowerment* best describes the positive impact of Black father presence because in any number of ways Black father presence empowers Black daughters to live their lives with confidence and a sense of achievement. Black women who are self-assured and have experienced success in vocational endeavors and relationships often attribute their success to the sustaining presence of their Black fathers.

Some women attribute their very survival to their involvement with their fathers. They describe a mutual dynamic in which the relationship between father and daughter was important for their mutual survival. In the relationship, daughters came to know that they were loved and valued. In the context of a racist society that often denigrates Blacks and thwarts their struggle to survive, the love, encouragement, and respect of a Black father for his Black daughter helps immunize her against the negative judgments that come her way on a daily basis. When American society presents the ideal image of what constitutes feminine beauty as white, blue-eyed, blond, straight-haired, with aquiline facial features, Black women need an alternative source of determining value that deems Black women attractive and desirable in spite of what the larger society suggests. The mortality rate for Black infants is twice that of white infants. The feminization and racialization of poverty contributes to the vulnerability of Black infants—boys and girls. Black fathers who provide for the nurture of their daughters help ensure their daughters' survival against the odds. It is clear that Black daughters need the presence of their fathers to help them survive.

How can Black daughters contribute to the survival of their fathers? Black daughters do so not in terms of material resources, but more in terms of emotional resources. The admiration and love of Black daughters for their Black fathers feeds the self-esteem needs of men for whom survival as free Black men is threatened. The need for Black fathers to provide certain emotional and relational gifts to their Black daughters instills in Black men a rea-son for being—a purpose in life. This mutual give-and-take between Black fathers and their daughters is present for fathers and daughters across racial and ethnic groups. What makes the issue one of survival is the heightened vulnerability that both Black daughters as infants and Black fathers as young men have in America. Black daughters and Black fathers need each other's adoring and concerned commitment in order to ward off chal-lenges to their ability to thrive and grow.

What are the gifts that Black fathers have to offer to their daugh-ters that make for empowered lives? One crucial gift is the instal-lation of the belief that their Black daughters belong. That belonging begins with a sense of being wanted. Black fathers who can communicate to their daughters that they were wanted, as opposed to being accidents or mistakes, assist their Black daugh-ters in feeling that their very existence is rooted in a wish that they have life and a space (place) within which to live that life. Planned or unplanned, born naturally or adopted, seen often or infre-quently, Black daughters need to hear from their Black fathers that they have a place in the life of their Black fathers. If Black fathers can communicate the message, "You belong to me and I belong to you," their daughters not only feel that they belong to their Black father in particular, but that they belong in general. Black daugh-ters will feel that a place in this world was desired for them and, therefore, that they deserve a place in it.

Ed Wimberly has written eloquently about the plight of many African Americans at the turn of the twenty-first century who are relational refugees.[10] They feel that they are unconnected to others and consequently live lonely, falsely self-sufficient, and empty lives. Without a sense of belonging and connectedness they live either isolated lives or lives that seek connection in the wrong ways or with the wrong things. One woman in the Wade-Gayles collection of stories characterizes this sense of belonging as the feeling her father gave her that she had a place at the welcome table. She means, that is, she had a seat at the welcome table of life. "For as long as I can remember, my father taught me a form of power that did not come out of the barrel of a gun. He taught me a 'resistance of the heart,' that fought any notions of inferiority."[11]

Counter to the feelings of being unloved and unworthy, Black fathers involved in the lives of their daughters provide their daughters with a sense of being loved and worthy. Just their very presence communicates to their daughters, "I like you and want to be around you." With this sense of being loved and being worthy, Black daughters have the confidence to demand love, respect, and encouragement from others. Instead of questioning whether they are deserving of such love, respect, and encouragement, Black daughters empowered by the loving presence of their Black fathers seek relationships with others in which there is mutual admiration, regard, and support. These confident women learn the differences between Black men and Black women, and understand those differences. Moreover, they learn what they are willing to accept from men. Their self-esteem is such that they will not tolerate degrading and abusive treatment. Such denigration of their personhood was neither modeled nor visited upon them, so they are predisposed not to accept it from Black men.

A Black daughter more easily learns what it means to be in relationship with a Black man if she had a Black father around while she was growing up. She learns how men communicate—how their linear thinking sometimes clashes unintentionally with the circular consciousness of most women. And with the abiding presence of her father, she learns that even when these clashes occur, they might be resolved in mutually affirming ways.

Black fathers teach Black daughters how to individuate. Nancy Chodorow[12] and the Wellesley College Centers for Women have informed all of us of the importance of connection in the emotional makeup of women. Yet there must be some capacity for individuation at those developmental stages when self-identity formation requires separation. As males for whom individuation and separation are more resident in the developmental pattern, Black fathers provide access to this other side of growth in relationship. This is especially true for those fathers whose continued presence reflects a value for connection even as they demonstrate the need to move away emotionally at times. At times the connection between mothers and daughters can become too intense, leading to conflict and hostility. Black fathers who can act as buffers without taking sides help mothers and daughters preserve their relationship in spite of the current upheaval in the connection.

Without access to a father, a Black daughter may experience men as a mystery. Cut off from involvement with the life of a significant male, the ways, movements, and perspectives of men are unknown and unfamiliar. Fatherless Black women are hurt by this lack of knowledge. Instead of knowing or having some sense of what men are like or what men want, they make guesses and choices that make life problematic for both men and themselves.

Much of what has been said about what Black fathers can mean to Black daughters is true for fathers and daughters in general. What makes the Black father-daughter connection so important is the monumental need for Black men and Black women to understand and live in loving relationship with one another. Having examined the attitudes that Black men and Black women have for one another, Orlando Patterson concludes that Black men and Black women are the most divided couples of all racial ethnic groups in the United States.[13] Black men and Black women are the most divorced and the least married. Consequently, one of the more important features of the Black father–Black daughter relationship is how Black women learn what it means to be in relationship with a Black man in positive and affirming ways. The emphasis here is on the affirmation of men of the same race. A supportive and nurturing relationship with a Black father can teach Black girls the following.

1. How to love a *Black* man
2. How to support *Black* men
3. How not to hate *Black* men
4. How not to feel abandoned by *Black* men
5. How to feel loved by *Black* men
6. How not to be afraid of *Black* men
7. How not to reject *Black* men
8. How not to dismiss *Black* men
9. How not to be in competition with *Black* men
10. How to feel supported and loved by *Black* men

To the extent that Black women look to Black men for lifelong partnership, caring and nurturing relationships with Black fathers early on in Black women's lives help Black women enter those relationships with Black men with greater courage and confidence. They are less likely to have the triple fears of rejection, abandonment, and commitment (the "triple fears" factor). They are less likely to function in those relationships with rage, anger, and depression (the "rad" factor).

Recognizing that God is neither male nor female, some women claim that their knowledge and experience of God has been expanded by their encounter with their fathers. It is not that God is male; nor that God has only male characteristics and attributes. Rather it is that in addition to the "feminine" side of God, these women have come to know God more fully through their encounter with the maleness of their fathers, which has contributed to seeing the "masculine" side of God. Without a father present this more comprehensive and complete picture and relationship with God would not be possible.

Does a father have to be there 24/7? That would be best. But more important than the amount of time is the consistency of the presence. The reliability of a father's interest has the capacity to make up for the lack of contact. Trusting that their fathers will be in their lives on a consistent and regular basis builds daughters' trust and confidence. It is when such reliable and consistent presence is maintained that even small portions of time spent together have an everlasting impression. Barras talks of such encounters as "morsels" from her father. The times together were not many, but they were powerful. Another writer refers to them as "pieces" from her father. These pieces had the capacity to be woven into a broadcloth of memories whose warmth and protection remain with her still.

Jennifer and Me

Part of the reason I was asked to write this chapter was because I am the father of a daughter. Jennifer is our only child, and so the relationship between us is one of a father whose only child is a daughter. We share that "onlyness." I decided that as a part of this chapter I would take the opportunity to talk with my daughter about our relationship. And since I am writing primarily about the experience of daughters and their fathers, I focused on Jennifer's thoughts and feelings about me. I gave her five sets of questions:

1. What would you say about your father? What kind of person is he? How would you describe him? What do you like most about him? What do you like least about him?
2. As a Black woman, what was important in your development in having a Black father?
3. How would you describe the relationship between you and your father?
4. What do you consider the most important features of a Black father for a Black daughter?
5. Is there anything more you think significant to say about Black fathers and Black daughters?

Jennifer's responses humbled me. In response to the first question, Jennifer described me as even-tempered, hardworking, dedicated, smart, and funny. I try to be as even-tempered as possible. I have seen what can happen in families, including my own, when persons go too far in the expression of their anger and frustration. I have witnessed the unintended consequences of impulsive behavior that lacked reason. These unintended consequences were often impossible to remedy, resulting in years of acrimony and sometimes death. I remember when I was ten years old watching as the body of a young man was brought through the alley on a stretcher out to a police van. His brother had shot him. A blanket was draped over the body, but a red stain where the bullet had entered had formed on the blanket. The brothers had been fighting over something trivial, and a gun was used to settle the argument. Early on in my own life I vowed to try to maintain an even temper so as to avoid being driven to actions that I might regret and be unable to make up for.

I was brought up with the old adage in the Black community that one had to be twice as good as whites in order to gain half the recognition one deserved. Moreover, I never considered myself as terribly smart, but found that working hard helped make up for the cognitive deficit. In second grade I was behind my peers in reading. When the reading segment of the class convened, I was relegated to a row for the slow readers. Embarrassed and ashamed, I was determined to extricate myself from that group.

With help from my father, I read my assignments over and over again until I became more comfortable with and confident in my reading. By third grade I was a "regular" reader. What I learned was that learning did not come to me easily but that with hard work I could achieve just about anything. My mother and father were married for thirty-six years before my mother died in 1973. My father worked for the Philadelphia Public Schools for twenty-nine years before he retired. Such commitment and fidelity made a strong impression on me. In addition to a proclivity for long-term commitments, I also have the capacity to stick with a task for very long periods of time. Jennifer and I often tease each other that this is one trait of mine she did not pick up. I like to stay with a task until it is done. I think this is what Jennifer meant when she referred to me as dedicated.

Jennifer considers me smart. This is because when she asks me a question I generally have knowledge about that which she is asking. Of course, when she was a child it was easy to demonstrate knowledge about things that sparked her curiosity. As an adult I think she seeks my advice about those things to which my experience has contributed to a certain amount of wisdom. In addition, I love to learn. I like having knowledge because it makes human existence much more interesting. With the belief that there are multiple ways to understand events and people in the world, I am motivated to learn as much as I can about the complex realities of life. I would be the first to tell you that I cannot tell a joke. In fact, it is very difficult for me to remember jokes. Very rarely do I include a humorous story in my sermons. So what is Jennifer referring to when she says I am funny? "We share a sense of humor," she states. This is true. Both Jennifer and I look to find the humor in any given situation. It is our way of taking the edge off the seriousness of everyday reality, which, absorbed without mediation of some sort, has the capacity to depress and lead to despair. We have had serious discussions—about life and death, confused identity, failed relationships, and other issues that border on ultimate concern—that have often ended in laughter. I remember a time when I had pneumonia and it was difficult for me to breathe. It was particularly painful for me to laugh. At nine years old, Jennifer thought it was the most riotous fun to tell a joke or to refer to something we had laughed about some time before and see me wracked with pain as I laughed. Cruel as it may have seemed, Jennifer and I shared a sense of humor that was reflected in this mixture of pain and laughter. Life is a mixture of joy and sorrow, crying and laughter. One without the other is only half a life. Each needs the other in order to fully appreciate the other. Yes, we share that sense of humor that seeks the absurdly humorous in the deadly serious as a way of preserving the fullness of life.

What Jennifer likes most is my level-headedness, my ability for critical thinking. She feels she can come to me and have me listen and help her see a solution. I do this in a rational, methodical way. She teases me that I often respond to questions by naming three things: one, two, three. It is always three things, as if the world and all of its information can be constituted in threes. Jennifer repeated that she likes my sense of humor, my even-temperedness. She finds my even-temperedness to be a good counterbalance to her mother, whose initial response to things is an emotional one. With what I perceive to be an indication of idealization, Jennifer reports that she has a sense that her Dad can do anything. She likes that I know about a lot of things. I have a lot of know-how and practical information. I rarely disappoint when consulted.

What does Jennifer like least about me? I did not set adequate limits for her when she was growing up. During her childhood she did not like having limits set and I tended to empathize too much with her discomfort with limits. When I was growing up, I resented how I was treated at times concerning limit setting. There was never any opportunity to make a case for myself. The response to any question that began with, "How come..." was, "Because I said so." Inside of me I vowed never to say that to any child of mine. And I never did, much to the regret of both Jennifer and me. She reports that it has made her adult life rockier. It is harder for her to accept limits in life, and she has set up a pattern of trying to find ways to get around things. She is aware of this tendency and works hard to avoid this approach to life. But it would be easier for her if we as parents had been better at setting limits.

Another thing that Jennifer likes least about me is that it is hard to get a dollar out of me. I am a penny-pincher. Being a penny-pincher can have its benefits, especially when she needs money, but overall Jennifer views me as excessively frugal. I would have to agree. In my defense, I must tell a story that my father often recited to me when I was growing up. It was just a few years after the start of the Great Depression. Between his junior and senior years in college he worked on campus. At times the food on campus was so meager that he would eat mustard sandwiches (two pieces of bread with only mustard between them). Another contributing factor to my frugality was the strategy a local bank in Philadelphia used to recruit customers at a young age. The Philadelphia Savings Fund Society would send an armored truck once a week to the public schools to collect the deposits of schoolchildren. This started when I was in fifth grade. It was a real treat to see my ten-cent- and twenty-cent-deposits add up and earn interest. I am not sure if Jennifer knows it or not, but the savings in that account were used to facilitate her mother's and my elopement. My frugality helped create the circumstances from which she was given life. Jennifer reports that I have gotten better, less "cheap." And she has become less of a spendthrift.

As Jennifer reflected on question number two, she found that as a Black woman it was important to have a father while growing up. Many of the Black women she knows now did not. Her experience of other Black women who grew up fatherless has been so prevalent that it has been striking to her that *her* father was present. Because her father was so high achieving it showed Jennifer what Black people could be and what she could be as a person. Her experience with a Black father offered a different perspective from that which was portrayed in the media. What she experienced with her father influenced what she was looking for in a husband. Jennifer believes she would have had a more dubious expectation of finding what she wanted in a husband if she had grown up fatherless.

Jennifer sees our relationship as close, but not sentimental. I would agree with her that I am not a touchy-feely, emotive person. However, Jennifer sees me as present, committed, devoted, and supportive. The part of Jennifer that is touchy-feely she got from her mother. To have gotten that from me would have been a miracle, given my family of origin. I grew up in a family that was not very affectionate. I rarely saw my mother and father hug or kiss. We just did not do that in my family, even between parents and children. The story that best illustrates this is the story of my going away to be a camp counselor one summer when I was in high school. My wife and I are high-school sweethearts, so we knew each other at the time of this send-off. In fact, my wife and her mother had come over to add their good-byes. When it came time to leave, I was on my way out of the door when my future mother-in-law said to me, "Homer, aren't you going to kiss your mother good-bye?" Both my mother and I had looks of embarrassment on our faces. I turned, went back, and gave my mother a kiss on the cheek, but it did not feel natural to me. In my marriage and with Jennifer I have tried to be more affectionate, but it does not come easily for me. I am glad that even though she has not experienced me as touchy-feely, Jennifer can still feel that we are "close."

Jennifer considers the most important feature of a Black father for a Black daughter to be *presence*. Black fathers should find ways of being present in the lives of their children, if not by staying married to their child's mother, then by finding other ways of being consistently present in their lives. Black fathers need to be supportive and protective. Anything else is icing on the cake. Most important, though, is presence—being there. The one other thing that Jennifer thought was significant to say was that Black fathers should make sure that their presence is a benefit, not a detriment. There should not be any abuse, neglect, or exploitation of their children. If a Black father is negatively influencing his family, he should get some help.

My daughter's additional witness to the impact of Black fathers on Black daughters highlights again the importance of presence. Without being present it becomes impossible for Black fathers to make the kinds of contributions to their Black daughters that will empower their daughters to thrive and live more abundant lives. Jennifer also speaks to the reality that presence alone is not enough. That presence should be experienced as supportive and protective. If it is not, then Black fathers are called upon to work on themselves (with professional help if necessary) in order to make positive contributions to the lives of their Black daughters.

I included some insight into my own background and personality as I reported on Jennifer's responses to my questions. The purpose was twofold: (1) how Black fathers present themselves in the lives of their children and families is deeply influenced by their own childhoods and the families in which they were raised. This is not new; we know this already. What is often overlooked, though, is the fact that father absence may be a learned response taught by virtue of the absence of a father in the home. What this means is that Black fathers who "choose" to be absent and who abandon their children may not always have a full range of options available to them from which to choose. The choice of emulating a father who is present is not readily available or accessible in the lived experience of many Black fathers. What Black boys need are Black men whose mere presence teaches, models, and makes available for appropriation a father identity that is committed, supportive, and protective. (2) Not all of what Black fathers bring to childrearing is ideal. No Black father can be perfect. There are ways in which Black fathers have learned what it means to be a Black father that need correction or guidance. Even in their efforts not to be the father that their father was to them, Black fathers can err in any number of different ways. What Black fathers need are mentor-coaches whose gentle intrusion into the lives of Black fathers affirms their fatherhood and offers support as they struggle with what is the best way to be present to their children.

What follows are two vignettes that speak to two of the dominant themes addressed thus far: consistent presence and the lingering effects of father absence. Both vignettes come from my pastoral counseling ministry.

Cheryl is a forty-year-old divorced mother of three girls. The girls' ages are nine, six, and three. Cheryl's mother and father divorced when she was ten years old. Although she and her mother moved across the country at the time of the divorce, Cheryl's father remained an active participant in her life. She would visit him or he would visit her at least once every two months, and every summer she spent a month with him. Cheryl's father was always available for telephone conversations with her and often took the initiative to call her in between their visits. He attended her graduations from high school and college.

Cheryl had been married for ten years before her divorce two years ago. The divorce was a bitter one. They fought over child custody, child support, and the division of property. Cheryl was awarded custody, but there was ample time and space provided for the girls and their father to get together. When her ex-husband began to renege on child support and failed to follow up on getting together with the girls on previously arranged visits, Cheryl entered into a mild depression. The experience with her ex-husband was directly opposite of the experience she had had with her father. It was not so much the financial strain or lack of relief from childrearing that bothered Cheryl most. What most bothered her was the impact her ex-husband's absence from the life of their girls was having on the girls. The girls' father would arrange to pick them up or visit them, but would often cancel, sometimes with a call of apology and sometimes with no call at all. The impact on the girls was negative, but in different ways. Charlene, the oldest, began to speak negatively about her father and began to act out in school. Charmaine, the middle girl, became withdrawn and quiet. In kindergarten she began to play by herself and did not interact with the other children. Lyn, the youngest, would often ask where her daddy was and would cry uncontrollably when her father did not show up when expected. At first, when their father would contact them, the girls would be very excited about getting together with him. Erratic though the get-togethers were, the girls looked forward with anticipation to seeing their father. His continued failures to follow through drained the enthusiasm of the girls. Recently they have begun to complain about having to get together with him.

In this situation we see both the enthusiastic joy that even less-than-consistent presence can create as well as the harmful effects of inconsistent presence. Because of Cheryl's experience with her own dad, she is able to refrain from talking about her ex-husband in derogatory ways with her girls. Much of my pastoral counseling is focused on supporting Cheryl in the face of her own disappointment with what has occurred in her marriage and helping with her struggle to sustain her daughters in the face of their disappointment in their father.

Lillian is a fifty-year-old woman who came to counseling asking the question, "Why do I find myself in so many relationships with men where I am taken advantage of?" Lillian has been divorced for twenty years. Over the past thirty years she has been involved in relationships with men where she has felt she has made wrong choices, resulting in a feeling on her part of having been used. The relationships usually begin well, with mutual regard and respect. But after a while Lillian begins to be accused of being selfish and self-centered. Physical and emotional abuse is often the punishment that she endures as a result of the displeasure her lovers expressed.

In the counseling we have focused on answering her original question. What has emerged is that Lillian establishes the relationship on an uneven basis. Where there seemingly is mutual give-and-take in the relationship, the reality is that Lillian is doing all of the giving and her lovers are doing all of the taking. When Lillian begins to sense that too much is going in the opposite direction, she pulls back. Oftentimes the sign of her having given too much takes the form of a financial calamity. The credit card she let her lover use is maxed out, the car she lent him disappears, she is unable to buy a house because her credit rating is so poor, and she eventually has to file for bankruptcy. When Lillian pulls back, her lovers resent her retreat and take their frustration and anger out on her through physical and emotional abuse. Further exploration reveals that Lillian feels she has to give more than she should in order to maintain the interest of her lovers. She fears that if she does not, they will leave. Rather than experience that rejection and abandonment, she gives and gives until the signs become clear that she is jeopardizing her own financial, physical, and emotional well-being.

Thus far in the counseling we have exposed this pattern and Lillian has begun to be more vigilant and more self-protective in her relationships. What has emerged recently is a wish on Lillian's part to talk about her relationships with her father. Lillian felt rejected by her father while she was growing up and could not do anything to please him or win his favor. Lillian believes she is playing out her wish to please and satisfy her father through her current relationships with men. Lillian and I have just begun to explore this avenue, but in light of what has been presented here, her conjecture is probably accurate. In both the case of Cheryl and that of Lillian we see the powerful effect of father absence on the development of personality and behavior.

The Church's Role in Preventing Father Absence

The Black church must make an aggressive effort to stem the tide of father absence. First and foremost, it must be father affirming and father friendly. Rather than castigate and judge fathers who have children out of wedlock or whose presence has been erratic, Black churches must welcome all fathers into the church and affirm their role as fathers to their children. Second, Black churches should offer spiritual support to fathers who seek to be present for their children. The community of faith as the embodiment of Christ should shower Black fathers with grace, mercy, forgiveness, and the good news that as they respond to the call on their lives to be good fathers, the mighty power of the Holy Spirit is with them. The love and encouragement of the church can go a long way in sustaining the patience and commitment fathers need to make in providing ongoing presence to their children. Finally, Black churches, as they are able, need to offer concrete resources to fathers in their efforts to make a faithful response to fatherhood. These resources can include information about parenting and child development. These resources can also include job training and employment opportunities. The Black church can provide counsel to Black fathers and mothers about how their relationship can be enhanced so as to create an environment of trust and safety for their children. In these and other creative initiatives the church undertakes the ministry of assisting fathers in being the abiding and life-giving presence that empowers Black girls to become the healthy and whole Black women God wants them to be.

CHAPTER SEVEN

Who Gives This Woman to Be Wed? Nurturing the Daddy-Daughter Relationship

While having my morning coffee at my neighborhood coffee shop, I engaged in casual conversation with an acquaintance who is also coffee shop regular. I had not been there for several weeks; so as casual acquaintances will sometimes do, I was asked how things were going. I shared that I had been away fishing for a couple of weeks. This was immediately met with the response, "I used to fish with my dad." The response sent my mind racing. I heard the response as more than a simple comment about fishing. It was more than a response that said, "I know about fishing." What I heard was a statement about an important relationship while growing up. Had this conversation simply been "guy talk," the sharing about fishing with Dad would have been simple sports talk; and most guys, at some level, engage in some type of sports talk. This conversation, however, was not "guy sports talk" because I was not talking to another guy. I heard the response as a significant childhood memory that expressed the importance of the daddy-daughter relationship.

If we listen, we will frequently hear the voices of adult daughters declaring the importance of their daddies in their lives. There are multiple statements of how close or how distant daughters are to daddies. Contained within those statements is another point that daughters will often make. Daughters will declare how vitally important a daddy is to the emotional and social health of a woman. A woman colleague in ministry has said to me on more than one occasion that it is vitally important that fathers become and remain close to their daughters. She says, "When the fathers are absent, you can see in the misguided behaviors of teenage girls just how much they desire the presence of their fathers in their lives." She continually declares how many young girls seek male attention to substitute for the attentive relationship that is desired with their fathers. Connecting this thought to a point from chapter 2—that is, fathers tend to ignore their daughters because of the preference for a son—the thought of a daughter's desire to overcome her feeling of having been rejected by her father makes perfect sense. Although we tend to place the greatest weight upon the strength of the mother-daughter relationship, we men should not continue to underestimate the power and importance of the daddy-daughter relationship.

Let's look at and talk about the ways we see and treat girls and women. We need to take a very close look at how we, African American men, view and understand the girls and women in our lives. I am a firm believer in the idea that says that what we believe about a person guides how we treat a person. So let's talk about what it is we believe about girls and women, and then about how we treat our daughters based on what we believe.

Labor Value

If we were to gather opinions about children within different cultures throughout the world, we would hear a fairly consistent voice on the importance and value of children. Even if we were to do a historical study, we would find that same consistent voice echoing over time. No matter which cultures we view, we tend to hear a consistent opinion on the value of girls and women. Unfortunately, to speak of value is not the same as speaking of importance. Girls and women have, for the most part, been viewed and valued as property. Whereas we have tended to promote independence in our boys, we have tended to promote dependence in our girls. We socialize girls to see themselves as whole beings only when they have been matched and mated with a man. A woman's value has tended to be seen in her labor. I mean this in both senses of the word as it applies to women. We have placed a high value on her domestic labor—the work she can do. We have also placed a high level of value upon bearing children, which is also called "labor."

These views have tended not to be any different within the male-preferred culture of the United States. Americans take great pride in affirming our history as the promotion of freedom, liberty, and justice for all. But African American girls and women have suffered deep humiliation in America by Americans. Although all women are confronted by the sex and gender challenges of America, African American women have endured a particularly unfortunate burden as a result of slavery in the United States. The humiliating actions and attitudes that African American girls and women have experienced at the hands of European American women and men have often been affirmed and intensified by the ways African American men relate to African American women and girls. In our deep American history, there is no doubt that African men and women alike were regarded as property without any human rights. But we should not conclude from that knowledge that there was no hierarchy in place. African women and men were valued differently, and the desired activity determined which one was more highly valued at any given moment.

African girls were always described in terms of their potential for pleasuring the landowner and their labor value. It is really quite disturbing to read auction materials from the slavery period of American history. There are frequent allusions to and declarations of African girls' and African women's ability to pleasure the landowner. Combined with that, there were always assertions of African women's ability to bear children to increase his holdings. She was always valued according to how much and what type of physical labor she could supply and endure in the house or the field. As we view girls and women today, how differently do we assess their value from the views that guided the exploitation of girls and women on the auction block? A close look at mass media and popular culture just might reveal an updated auction block that exploits and demeans girls and women. Men, young and old, look at a woman and immediately determine how much physical pleasure she will be able to give us. Next, we think about her labor, that is, her ability to take care of our castle and call us "Sire." And there is no question—she had better produce a son! For the most part, our general attitudes remain the same: girls and women are property.

Blood for Sale

Many of us have grown up with the understanding that "blood is thicker than water." The statement, of course, says that "blood" relationships, which are family relationships, are vitally important relationships. The meaning of this saying used to suggest that little or nothing could separate family ties. Along with this was the idea that while many relationships are expendable, you never sell out your family—that is, you never sell out your blood. In a different time, African American men greeting one another affirmed this idea. In days gone by, it was not unusual to hear greetings like, "What's up, Blood?" "Blood" expressed a deep relational connection. It was an identification of respect and brotherhood. Acknowledging one another as "Blood" spoke a recognition of a shared experience in America. It spoke that we knew the same struggle and would survive by supporting one another as blood bound together. This acknowledgment meant that family was not limited to a traditional understanding of family ties dependent on having the same birth parents and growing up in the same household. Calling another "Blood" declared a spiritual and social connection of unity, which was also unifying. Even the African American flag interpreted this connection. The colors of the flag are red, black, and green. The color red has been interpreted as representing the blood of the people. Consequently, identifying another Black man as "Blood" was a declaration of promise, support, and life. There was also an intergenerational statement associated with blood that spoke to a social dynamic of respect and responsibility. Black men regularly identified Black boys and young men as "Young Blood." Contained in this identification was a commitment to mentor the next generation.

The tragedy of this identification is the fact that "Blood" as a term of respect and family connectedness only applies to boys and men. Among men, nonblood has been identified as blood and honored as brothers; but that is the extent of the social acknowledgment. For as much as we recognize blood as family, we have had a different relationship with girls and women as our blood. Of course, we have acknowledged the connection and identified Black girls and women as our sisters. "Sister," like the connection of "Blood," also includes nonblood relations. Yet, as a term of endearment and social connectedness, the term "Blood" has not been transferred and has not related to girls and women. "Blood" has been limited to a man's greeting of other men. What does this say about our views of girls and women? What effect has only calling men and boys "Blood" had on our relationships with girls and women?

During the years when the idea of blood was most popular, I don't ever remember hearing girls and young women referred to as "Blood" in the context of social greetings. There have been terms to identify girls and women as family, but blood as a very essential way of identifying girls and women with respect and as family relatives has been absent. Has this meant we have not seen our sisters as possessing a "blood thicker than water"? Too often, we have seen our sisters as less important, and therefore, as not being our blood in the struggle in the same way as we have seen men as blood. While we might see the color of our skin as promoting a sense of family connection, a significant part of our relationships with girls and women seems not to be defined by blood. In fact, more times than not, it seems that the blood of our girls and women has been for sale. It is as though we have gone to the blood bank and cashed in on our daughters as a commodity to be traded rather than maintaining a close relationship. Our daughters have been seen as less important and sold because our sense of family legacy and inheritance is passed on from father to son. Many of us have sold our daughters because they have not been a source of pride the way sons have been by affirming our manhood. Our daughters have been sold—and sold out—because in many ways they have been seen as family property instead of blood relatives.

Love for Sale

Historically speaking, families entered into very sophisticated financial negotiations to determine whom their daughters would marry and at what price. The family—either the bride's or the groom's—received a dowry or a bride-price to pay for her to be given and received. The dowry was money, goods, or estate given *by* the parents of the bride to the husband. The bride-price was money, goods, or estate given *to* the parents of the bride by the husband. In either case, the daughter was part of a business transaction that had nothing to do with securing her future comfort. The purchase price was always blood for sale. It is thought that many infant girls were killed so that the parents could avoid paying a dowry in the future. And, in the case of the bride-price, the young man sometimes had to work very hard in order to raise the funds to purchase his bride. This is what we saw happening in the biblical story of Jacob. Jacob worked fourteen years for Laban so he could marry Laban's daughter, whom he loved (read Genesis 29:16-30).

This very old practice of buying a wife has gone by different names but has endured for thousands of years. I recall visiting with friends in South Africa. A man I met at a social gathering there told me how expensive it was for him to get married. The expression on his face communicated the anguish from the experience of gathering all that the family of his intended required for him to be able to marry their daughter. And if we think these "payment" practices have not continued in one way or another, think again! Although the practice has to some degree changed, most of us still carry in our minds that it is the responsibility of the bride's family to pay the total cost of the wedding. We also tend to hold that it is the groom's responsibility to pay for the rehearsal dinner. These practices are the dowry and bride-price updated.

Today, more and more couples are paying for their entire wedding experience. In spite of this fact, we continue to look at the man who has several daughters as having the burden in his future of "paying for all those weddings." We sometimes describe the wedding experience by saying, "We are not losing a daughter. We are gaining a son!" Considering the history of seeing girls as property and sons as preferred, the saying can have a double meaning. The positive meaning could be: "Our daughter is our blood, a connection that will never be broken." The negative meaning could be: "We are getting the son we always longed for." While we do not tend to consciously think of our daughters as property, our connection to the tradition of viewing girls as property continues to support treating them as such.

Wedding Preparations

In days gone by, viewing girls as property was a given. Because men preferred sons, daughters became a means to an end. They became a means to financial security. Also, since there has been such an emphasis on the biblical image of women being saved by childbirth, and on the image of the virtuous woman as the one who takes care of the house and her family, we men can see, once again, how we have tended to value women for their labor. We have directed their development and social instruction to be focused on preparing them to labor as wives and mothers. Women were not encouraged to believe they had any authority over their own bodies, but like property their bodies were to be used for their "owner's" pleasure. This is why "obey" and "submission" have historically been such important concepts imposed upon women. And because male preference continues to be at the center of the culture, this is why those concepts continue to reign within our consciousness. Preparing daughters for life meant preparing daughters for a life of servitude. This attitude focused on preparing daughters for marriage as a house of bondage rather than encouraging marriage to be experienced as a bonding relationship.

We want to believe we have come so far as a society, but there are so many degrading traditions we continue to maintain. The larger society in which we live continues to socialize girls in the earliest days of their lives to look forward to marriage as their highest goal. The fairy tales that promote "happily ever after" shape young girls to prepare themselves to marry the prince who will rescue them. Girls learn very early that they are to look forward to marriage with great anticipation. One of the problems with the fairy tale is that boys are not socialized to anticipate marriage with great expectation the way girls are. Boys are conditioned to see marriage as a trap set for them. The dual message is that marriage promotes happiness, but marriage does not make boys happy. What develops from this is an attitude that says girls must learn what makes boys happy.

The lessons and messages we tend to teach girls put them in a double bind. The double message says marriage is good for girls but bad for boys. Boys are socialized to always rescue girls; and girls are socialized to always submit to a rescuing prince.

Furthermore, since marriage is defined as what makes girls happy, girls are taught they should learn how to make boys happy in marriage. None of these messages are the lessons we should teach girls or boys. How do we promote positive self-regard and self-esteem in a world that tends to identify women as second class? One effort has been to promote an identity of daughters being princesses. This effort, of course, has its strengths and weaknesses. On the positive side, encouraging daughters to see themselves as princesses promotes a sense of the regal that says they deserve the very best. On the less positive side, encouraging daughters to see themselves as princesses does not promote a sense of equality of being because the princess is never seen in the fairy tale as being as important as the prince.

During a family vacation, we were out shopping in an area that was very festive. There were a lot of sidewalk cafés, and music filled the air. My daughter got into the festive spirit by dancing as we walked down the street. Another shopper watching her dance along our way said to her, "You go, Girl!" To this, my daughter replied, "I'm not a girl; I'm a princess!" With all of us laughing, the stranger replied, "My apologies. You go, Princess!" My daughter was five at the time. I was so proud of her! Although she knew she was a girl, she was insistent on communicating that she was no ordinary girl. I was very proud of her insistence that she be addressed appropriately. But recognizing the limitations of the image of princess, I wondered what other image might be appropriate for her growth and development.

While there are those of us who will identify our daughters as "Princess" in an effort to promote a positive self-image, our society still tends to regard the princess as a distant second to the prince. And even when we encourage our daughters to go to college, there is often an underlying message that she should go to college to find a good husband. There are, of course, more women today who see their lives as not being defined by marriage; yet those women often bear the burden of being social outcasts. The woman who chooses not to marry is regularly seen as having too many issues, as being bitter, or as having "unnatural" desires. In short, the pressure for a woman to marry is so great that if she does not she is seen as having something wrong with her.

Give and Get

If there is a wedding day, the wedding ceremony in the Black church tends to support the tradition of girls being property. The drama and pageantry reinforces the ancient ideas of daughters as the property of their fathers and the wedding as a financial transaction that transfers property from one man to another. Tradition is strong; and the attitudes that sustain tradition are very strong. If we are going to change the unfortunate attitudes we have about our daughters, we must reimagine our ideas of tradition and change the rituals that promote the abuse of our daughters. We must change the wedding ceremony, which is an important image for marital life.

Let's review the dynamics of the wedding. At the beginning of the wedding ceremony, the groom walks out accompanied by the minister and the best man. There, the groom waits patiently for the entrance of the bride. The bride, however, takes the long walk, escorted down the aisle, to be presented as a gift to the groom. At her entrance, everyone stands in honor of her as the center and reason for the gathering. This is "her" day, the day she has been awaiting her whole life.

After acknowledging God's presence and stating what God has ordained by marriage, there comes that all-important question that reveals the ceremony to be a property transaction. The question: "Who *gives* this woman to be married to this man?" For a father to answer the question with the words "I do" means that the terms of the engagement contract—dowry or bride-price—have been fulfilled, and he approves closing the deal. How else could he give unless he acknowledges a sense of ownership over what he is giving to another? Although we may now see this giving as giving consent to the marriage, or as a father giving up his parental responsibility to provide for his daughter, the traditional meaning was the transfer of property.

Do you need more evidence of a traditional wedding being a financial transaction? Consider this: has anyone ever asked, "Who gives this man to be married to this woman?" No, never! If a groom ever heard such a question, he would no doubt respond, "Why are you asking that question? I'm not a punk! I'm my own man." A groom is automatically assumed to be his own person, not the property of his parents, whereas a bride is thought to belong to her father. As a result, when I am the minister at a wedding, I never ask, "Who gives this woman?" I approach the moment as a moment that says that she presents herself in marriage, just as he presents himself in marriage. Within my own wedding ceremony, my wife's father did escort her down the aisle; but my mother also escorted me down the aisle. There was no question asked regarding who gave whom. The ritual of our parents escorting us was one of several moments that represented the wedding ceremony as a union of individuals and families.

Because of the give-and-get attitude that has dominated the traditional understanding of weddings and marriage, it is essential that we change the way we nurture and socialize our daughters. We absolutely need to stop living into the ancient history of viewing girls as property to be used and abused by others. Furthermore, our history of slavery in the United States should truly encourage us to do all we can to change the give-and-get attitude and affirm our full humanity as people of African descent. Under slavery, we all were property. The last thing we should want to do is support degrading attitudes that continue to promote girls and women as property without rights or dignity. This is a change that must begin with fathers changing their minds and hearts about how they feel as fathers of daughters.

God created humanity in God's own image as male and female. Your daughter bears your image and likeness as much as your son does. And if you have no son, you still have a phenomenal gift from God in your daughter. Preparing her for life should not be understood as preparing her for marriage. We should give time and attention to the development of daughters by cultivating a relationship of openness and trust, just as we would with a son. We must nurture the image of God within girls through affirming the beauty and dignity of their very beings and not grounding their sense of self in labor. This also means not relating to daughters as we would to sons. Fathers have been known to relate to daughters as they would to sons in order to establish any measure of closeness. But substituting a father-son relationship by relating to a daughter like a son only tends to communicate how much more love her father would have for her if she were a boy. Being in relationship with our daughters means learning how to nurture them in the fullness of their being as girls who will grow into women. That sometimes means doing those things that test Black masculinity.

Having a conversation with another African American man as one father of a daughter to another, we began to share the importance of our being closely related and actively involved in our daughters' lives. His daughter being much older than mine, he began to ask me about my ability to care for my daughter in the absence of her mother. One of the critical indicators for him was wrapped in the question, "Can you do hair?" "Doing hair" has never been considered a very manly thing to do. As a result, this very simple question goes right to the core of what it means for African American men to father daughters. This is not a question of whether we take our daughters to the beauty salon, which might also be a challenge. The question did not just ask if I had the patience and took the time to help my daughter look good for the world; it also asked if I sought to develop the intimate relationship with my daughter that is a part of "doing hair." The challenge of doing hair means fathers enter their daughters' world and do not just expect daughters to enter the world of boys and men.

Because I was the primary caregiver for my daughter's earliest stages of development, I knew quite a bit about what was at the heart of the brother's question. I gave my daughter her first diaper change and her first bath. She slept on my chest, listening to my heartbeat, during her first days of life in this world. I answered her cries through the night and comforted her infant fears. I endured all of her immunization shots at the doctor's office, crying more than she did with every needle injection. When she learned how to stand and took her first steps, I was there. I fulfilled all of the traditional mothering roles in my daughter's life. As she has grown, I have continued to nurture her development by cooking with her. I have helped her learn her routines for her dance recitals. I taught her how to ride a bike, and cheered for her at school performances. I have shopped with her as well as for her. And yes, I have also practiced with her as she prepared for her karate-belt tests. A father must participate in every aspect of his daughter's life.

Daddy-Daughter Date Night

The daddy-daughter relationship must be cultivated in public as well as in the home. Some communities support the cultivation of the daddy-daughter relationship by hosting "Daddy-Daughter Date Night." This tends to be a semiformal event that includes dinner, entertainment, and dancing. This event is very much a family and community event. Hairstyling salons tend to be filled with mothers who have taken their daughters to have their hair styled for the evening. Nails get done. New dresses are purchased. There are many mothers who encourage, support, and affirm this event.

Participating in a social gathering of this nature helps say that the entire community supports and values the daddy-daughter relationship. The experience is affirming to fathers because they are gathered as a group to witness the importance of loving their daughters. The experience is affirming to daughters because in the company of their friends and other girls they have never met, their daddies attend to them. Furthermore, they are able to show off their daddies. This experience prepares girls for the world in a way a mother-daughter night out cannot. It is important for daddies to spend quality time out with their daughters, and these community events are a wonderful way to move toward changing the culture of daughters as property and promoting the importance of fathers nurturing their daughters. A photograph is often taken to help sustain the memory for a lifetime.

Biblical Character Study

To explore these dynamics, let us reconsider the Judges 11 story of Jephthah and his daughter. Jephthah's story is one of the few daddy-daughter stories we find in Scripture. The story is, however, a tragic story that leads us to challenge the views many men have about their daughters. Not only does the story challenge men's views of their daughters, the story also forces us to examine God's view of daughters. We know that neither the Bible nor the Christian tradition has been very affirming of women. Only a few women have been held in high esteem within the biblical record. The story of Jephthah and his daughter highlights the history of sons being preferred to daughters.

Jephthah was an outsider among the people. His father's name was Gilead. Jephthah was not the son of his father's wife. When Gilead's wife bore sons, Jephthah, like Ishmael, was kicked out of the household of his father by his brothers. He was deemed to be unworthy to inherit his father's possessions, and therefore he was not welcome among his father's people. Being unwelcome as a son of his father, he lived outside the community with the love of his daughter, his only child. The story suggests that Jephthah loved his daughter and had a very close relationship with her.

When Israel went to war against the Ammonites, the people of Gilead came to Jephthah and urged him to become captain of their army and lead them into battle against the Ammonites. It is funny the way those who are undesirable within the community become so desirable as warriors when the going gets tough within the nation. Jephthah negotiated with the elders of Gilead. His condition for fighting was that if he returned to Gilead to lead the people, he would return as the head of their army and leader of all the people of Gilead. Whereas he was once chased out of Gilead with nothing, he returned to become leader of all. Furthermore, it is so interesting to see how willing he was to embrace and fight for those who had denied his very being. Why do so many long to identify with, and become a part of, the very ones who hate them? More importantly, what is the cost to us for selling our souls to those who hate us?

Jephthah accepted the invitation of the elders of Gilead. But before going to war, he made a vow to God saying that whoever came out of the doors of his house to meet him upon his victorious return, he would sacrifice. This vow suggests that his concern for being victorious and returning to Gilead outweighed his thoughts for his own household. Typically, the women would come forth dancing upon the victorious return of the warriors.

Consider what happened after the Egyptians drowned in the Red Sea. Miriam, with tambourine in hand, began to dance with many women following her to celebrate the victory over the enemy of the people. Believing that one of his women servants would emerge from his house first, Jephthah vowed to sacrifice her to God. How could Jephthah believe that God would be pleased with a human sacrifice instead of a lamb or bull upon the altar? Jephthah's willingness to sacrifice a woman from his household is no different than the Levite in Judges 19 who sacrificed his wife. Only, in this instance Jephthah sacrificed his daughter as the price to be paid in order to have a home among the people who despised and rejected him.

Aside from the fact that Jephthah was more than willing to sacrifice a woman to fulfill his desire for acceptance, I wonder if he would have been so willing to sacrifice his only child had his child been a son? Of course, this question causes us to turn to the story of Abraham and his son Isaac. Abraham was also very willing to sacrifice his son Isaac on an altar beneath the knife. But in Abraham's case, the child sacrifice was unacceptable, and a ram in the bush was provided as an acceptable sacrificial offering to God. Why wasn't an animal provided for Jephthah to sacrifice in the place of his daughter? Like Jephthah, too many African American men are all too willing to sacrifice their daughters for personal gain. Our daughters have been lamenting and wailing for far too long. We must redefine our lives and our purpose in life to include the well-being of our daughters.

PART III

Wisdom from Fathers

CHAPTER EIGHT

Extended Fatherhood: Fathers, Grandfathers, Godfathers, and Pastor-Mentor Fathers

Affirmation Litany

Leader: *Human beings were the height of the creative process. God shaped the Black man in His image from the richest dark soil of the earth, and breathed into the man Life. Thus, man became a living, virtuous soul. Created in the image of God, the measure of a man is the extent to which he reflects God. God is firm, but He is also compassionate. God is strong, but He also cries. God is the provider, but He also appreciates receiving. God builds, and yet He embraces.*

Men: *We stand together in this worship service to affirm our noble African past, draw strength to confront the challenges of our present, and renew our vision for our future.*

Leader: *A vital relationship with Jesus the Christ is the necessary ingredient for a productive life. It is by following the footsteps of the Master that our worth as men is validated each day.*

Men: *It is our faith in Jesus that gives us the strength to build today for tomorrow. He improves the quality of our relationships. He provides guidance for us to act with sacrificial love for family, friends, and the stranger within our gate. He nurtures our lives, causing us to summon laughter to chase away the dull or disdainful moment.*

Leader: *We renew ourselves daily in prayer,*

Men: *In the study of God's Word, and laboring for the extension of God's Kingdom here on earth through our church, community, and global outreach.*

All: *We covet the prayers of all who listen that we continue to follow the Master's example: assist in liberating every woman so that her God-given potential be actualized; produce a healthy environment for our children to grow strong, proud, compassionate, and wise; remain steadfast in the knowledge that it is more important to lay down our lives daily. Amen.*

Joseph Hickman and Lee Butler
June 1988

Written more than twenty years ago, the above litany was developed to encourage churchmen to covenant together as men while affirming the importance of having commitments that are larger than our individual selves. We wanted to encourage men to live a definition of manhood that reflected commitments to family and community. The litany affirms the importance of spirituality and faith as vital to manhood, and the promotion of responsibility in relationship as essential to manhood. The litany affirms African American manhood to be most appropriately understood as godly, as we live together in community. This chapter presents four manifestations of African American manhood that can encourage new ways of understanding African American men in relationship and can aid in the future development of the African American community.

Success in White and Black

The standard image of success in the United States, most often characterized by annual income and material possessions, has been a white male image. Without a doubt, there have been African American images of success, but the most common images have been the products of popular culture, such as athletic and musical entertainers. As a result, the popularized road to success for African Americans has been entertainment, with other professional

118

paths regarded as inappropriate for Black men. For this reason, it has not been uncommon for African Americans to criticize an African American's career goals and accomplishments unrelated to entertainment with the words, "You're trying to be white." This criticism has only been rivaled by the assessment that a successful Black man has to marry a white woman, his "trophy wife," as the final indicator of his success. These very common assessments were expressed when Senator Barack Obama was elected president of the United States. Early in his campaign bid for the White House, he was confronted with the challenge of "not being Black enough." In addition to Mrs. Michelle Obama being identified (without any qualifying statements) as not being suited to be the nation's first lady, there were many statements regarding her being unmistakably African American as the wife of a successful Black man. Mrs. Obama's beauty challenges the stereotype of a success-ful Black man being partnered with a light-skinned Black or white woman.

The die has been cast! The idea that the image of success must be white has not been limited to the African American community. I have, from time to time, taught courses at colleges and universities while teaching at the seminary. Some years ago, a European American woman, who was registered for one of those university classes I taught, met with me at my seminary office. I had several pictures of my wife around my office. After a short time in the office, she commented, "I'm glad to see you are married to an African American woman. A lot of successful Black men marry white women, and then Black women lose out on the benefits of Black men's success." She then proceeded to tell me about her son's African American friends who would only date white women. Her sharing revealed the extent to which this prominent image of suc-cess as an awareness and criticism crosses racial lines. It is not unusual to hear African American women say that a Black woman will support a Black man to help him succeed; then when he is suc-cessful, he will leave the Black woman, who has sacrificed her all, for a white woman.

The success for an African American man is judged by income and material possessions. Because the standard has stereotypically been a white male image, the unfair assessment is that African American men must become white or, through entertainment, acquire the income and material possessions considered the marks of success, which might include marrying a white woman. For centuries, there has been an image of a white woman as the paragon of beauty and virtue, exalted on a pedestal. Viewing a woman—any woman—as an object, and identifying her as a prize on a pedestal, is a deep psychological challenge that we must work to overcome. Now that we have our first African American president of the United States, will we have to totally rethink our images of success? Time will truly tell. Certainly, we can live with more hope; but one person in a key position does not mean everything has changed forever.

An Overview of Success in the United States

The notion that the United States has been a white male-preferred society has meant the primary measurement of social benefits and social mobility has been the white male in a white-collar career. The critical marker for distinguishing those who have from those who have not has been the white male. Of course, white men do not all hold white-collar jobs, but that does not change the fact that the white male has been established as the standard image of success. Life, liberty, and the pursuit of happiness—the basic pillars of the American dream—have often been translated to mean a house, marriage, family, and a salary sufficient to provide all the creature-comfort resources to go wherever and do whatever *he* desires. Those are the signs that declare that a person is truly living the dream of America. These translated signs have all been indicators of privilege and upward mobility. Unfortunately, we have lived in a society that has not always sought to affirm these privileges for everyone within the United States.

There is an old adage that says, "Do as I say, not as I do." The adage declares a qualitative difference between words and actions. Although America has emphasized equality for its citizens, African American men have been acted against in ways that have ensured inequality between white and black. Although we have moved from noncitizenship to citizenship without full rights to citizenship with full rights under the law, our experience of citizenship under the law has consisted of hearing words that have not matched actions. There are doors we have been told are open to us only to discover the doors have been sealed shut from the inside. Then when we have acted to force open the door that we have been told is our entrance to advancement, we have been identified as aggressive and violent and inappropriate to occupy the space on the inside. Our experience with the adage as it has related to the benefits of citizenship has been "separate and unequal."

The Impact of American Slavery

During the antebellum period of U.S. history, it was illegal for Africans in America to be wed. And it was not until 1967 that miscegenation laws were struck down, allowing African Americans to marry persons of other races. Whereas marriage has been a human right and a right of citizenship, Africans in America have a history of having been denied full rights to marriage and having been denied the legal rights and protections afforded families formed by marriage. In these ways, Africans in America have been deprived of the full rights and privileges of citizenship. This must be understood in order to have a full picture of the positive and negative features of African American manhood.

Throughout the history of the United States, life, liberty, and the pursuit of happiness have not been social ideas supported by the political process exclusively. They have also been religiously and theologically supported ideas supporting the political process. Life, liberty, and happiness have been sought after as the privileges of citizenship. As such, legislation has supported and protected those privileges through laws on marriage—which has been inseparable from family—and property. And in those instances where there has not been actual legislation to prohibit African Americans from owning property, there have often been de facto laws, such as redlining, to prevent African Americans from purchasing what their money could have bought. Furthermore, too often, we have been forced to pay excessive prices for basic goods and services, which has meant we have not been able to accumulate wealth like other communities. Consequently, and to the detriment of African American men, the prominent political-theological perspectives on marriage, family, and property ownership have often done more to traumatize than to support African American manhood.

The American system of chattel slavery had a devastating impact on the formation of African American manhood. There is no denying that it was within slavocracy that white men became the image and model for success. Slavocracy is a national system of exploitation dedicated to keeping a group enslaved. The system defines people's lives and relationships through the use of politics and economics. The system defines and divides people, not just in terms of haves and have-nots, but also by politicizing every national relationship to determine social status and what is deemed socially appropriate. Every thought and action within slavocracy is, therefore, an effort to maintain the bondage of those identified as slaves.

Black men were thought and taught to be slaves for life, while white men were thought and taught to be human beings in God's image. The biblical book of Genesis declares that a man should leave his father and mother and cleave to his wife. This was possible for a U.S. citizen during the period of slavery; but this was not possible for an enslaved African. The enslaved African often experienced the cleaver and was separated from his wife. He had no rights as a citizen. The very fact that his family was broken up by the auction block, and marriage was made illegal for him, communicated both politically and theologically that manhood was unattainable for Africans in America.

American slavocracy declared enslaved Africans to be less than human. Ultimately, this meant that African Americans had no civil or human rights whatsoever. The system did everything it could to deny African American males the benefits of manhood. Those degradations distorted manhood and made it an inequitable ideal. Manhood is often measured by family relationships. So that they would never see themselves as being men like European American men, enslaved African men were not permitted to guide, guard, or protect their families. Consequently, the auction block was as much about power and separating African husbands from their wives and children as it was about commodity exchange.

Given our oppressive and unjust history as African American men struggling to be honored as men, it is imperative that we reestablish the terms of our living. The intentional attacks on the extended African family combined with the legal, sociopolitical, and religious bias of American society for a patriarchal nuclear family structure are strong reasons for the overwhelming negative assessment of African American manhood. These are the significant influences that have contributed to the deteriorated image of African American manhood and have provoked the challenges faced by the African American community on the whole. We can no longer afford to allow these atrocities of the past to define our present and our future. I believe it is essential that we revive the resistance tradition that motivated us in spite of the atrocities. As an example, when the law made it illegal for us to marry, we swept the law aside, jumped the broom, and declared ourselves to be husbands and wives. We must once again define our own future.

Finding a New Way

America has often defined leadership in terms of family headship. The federal tax identification of "head of household" is a significant identification. When telephone solicitors call, they regularly ask if they are speaking to the head of the household. When the qualities of public figures are generally described, the description often includes statements about family life. Marriage and family are thought to communicate a man's level of responsibility in life and to communicate his commitments to community health. Marriage and family are, therefore, thought to be attributes of leadership. This is why the tone of the historic 1965 document "War on Poverty Report" was so devastatingly critical of the African American family and community. In that government-authorized investigative report, Daniel Moynihan asserted that problems in the African American community were attributable to a breakdown in the nuclear family. This analysis was based, of course, on an assumption that alternative family structures developed by African Americans were deviant because they did not mirror the patriarchal nuclear family structure deemed healthy by the American political system. The voice of this document continues to echo through time and to influence how African American manhood is assessed.

So powerful is this reverberating voice that even when African American families adopt a nuclear patriarchal form, they have, time and time again, been judged negatively. It seems that no matter how we have tried to be approved, we have been kept on the outside and considered a deviant people. This attitude was expressed in many polls when President Obama was running for office. Polls stated over and over that many of the negative images of African Americans were still alive and influential. This is another example of how slavocracy has continued to affect our lives. Over the years, our humanity has been challenged by perverted laws and supremacist values that promote a traditional nuclear image of family, which to our mind's eye we can never seem to match. Family headship is not a bad thing to aspire to; however, we must select the appropriate image to inspire our actions.

The extent to which the United States has been a male-preferred society has meant that the link between African American manhood and community advancement has been unavoidable. Hence, African American manhood has always been associated with the advancement of the African American community as we have journeyed toward becoming full citizens of the United States of America. Religious and civic leaders exercised community responsibility and thereby established models of manhood for all African American men. This has been true since the earliest expressions of resistance within African American life. Throughout the years, these models have evolved and developed, yet the basic foundation has remained consistent because it is grounded in the fundamental values of family and community. I believe if we aspire to model our manhood after fatherhood, grandfatherhood, and godfatherhood while exemplifying the spirit of the pastor-mentor who understands that life and love are larger than any single self, we will radically reform ourselves and redefine our future.

Classic Images of African American Manhood

In order to offer new images for declaring African American manhood, I want to briefly review the classic images that continue to influence our formation into manhood. The dominant images that came out of the early 1940s and after World War II can be seen in the classic debate between Booker T. Washington and W. E. B. DuBois. The intellectual positions and personal presentations of both these men helped them become the role models who defined and influenced African American male development for their generation and the generations that followed. Both men epitomized leadership by emphasizing activities that would lead the African American community into full citizenship with all rights and privileges. Although neither man emphasized fatherhood as part of his plan for advancement, their concerns for the integrity of the African American community had fatherly and mentoring overtones. They both emphasized strength of character, a strong work ethic, and a deep commitment to African American people. Neither man was driven by individualism or materialism.

The dominant images that came out of the 1950s and the Civil Rights struggle can be seen in the classic positions held by El-Hajj Malik el-Shabazz (a.k.a. Malcolm X) and the Reverend Doctor Martin Luther King, Jr. Both of these men loved their children and struggled to make America a land where all children could live with dignity. They both stressed the importance of character for social uplift. They exemplified courage as a prerequisite for confronting social injustice. Their life stories, which reveal the origins of their commitments, demonstrate the importance of men mentoring boys to men. Both their fathers were pastors who were committed to mentoring and community empowerment. The individual stories of King and Malcolm X declare that imperfect men can be transformed to become reformers and leaders among men. In the words of Ozzie Davis at the funeral of Malcolm X, "Malcolm was our manhood, our living, Black manhood... [and] our own Black shining prince!" Scripture declares, "Where there is no vision, the people perish" (Prov. 29:18 KJV). King inspired us to dream dreams and to see a new vision. The lives Shabazz and King lived were as men of faith. The commitments they held, for which they died, exemplified the importance of the spirit and the fact that living humanly to inspire others is more important than seeking individual gain. They lived and died loving us with their entire beings.

From Classic to Contemporary Images of African American Manhood

I believe it is important that we recover the classic ideas of model manhood as we continue to press toward a new image of African American manhood. To the extent that I am advocating the recovery of old ideals, I am suggesting that the new image we develop will be guided by the very best of who we have always been. On the whole, we have struggled to be men of distinction. Although we have been stereotyped as lazy, we have worked hard to establish ourselves as proud men to be respected. Unfortunately, as we have sought to establish ourselves, we have had to contend with oppressive forces that have caused many of us to turn from fatherhood to sirehood, and from fighting for justice to fighting among ourselves. True manhood is about growth and change through learning to surrender to the power of life by resisting the destructive power of death. Our emphasis on sirehood is the result of a perverted focus on prowess and pleasure as the power of life. Sirehood must be reformed into an energy that honors the prowess of leadership by taking pleasure in the ways the community benefits from our giving for the growth and benefit of others. Fatherhood is the celebration of life that promotes the goodness of fair and equitable distribution of life's benefits.

We are living in an age of new challenges. Although we continue to be affected by the past and our assessment of the ways past practices affect our daily lives, we must acknowledge the ways racial consciousness has changed in America. We have moved from being a strongly racialized society divided into black and white, to a belief that America had become a colorless society with more tolerance, to America as a "salad bowl" with multicultural diversity. Today, we are living with an unusually strong desire to declare America as being a "postracial society." We hear this pronouncement coming from both whites and Blacks. The nomination, election, and inauguration of the forty-fourth president of the United States of America, Barack Hussein Obama, the first African American president, have been identified as evidence that we have overcome and are now living in a postracial society. Embodying the old and presenting the new, Obama represents, for many, a new model of manhood. By virtue of his career path and his office, we know that he is committed to community and the nation. His commitment to his marriage and family are unmistakable. But is he evidence that all the sins of the past have been atoned and we are able to live in full liberty?

Since the inauguration of President Obama, the nation has declared: "See! We are a postracial society. King's dream has been fulfilled! This is proof that the Civil Rights struggle was a success, that racism has been conquered in the United States, that we *have* overcome." However, if this is so, and racism has been conquered, why did assassination threats against Obama set a new record high when he became president-elect? Why did hate crimes and threats of racial violence escalate with the ages of the voices, ranging from elementary-school-aged children through middle-aged adults, all of them calling for Obama's assassination? Why did we see burning crosses and hanging nooses across this nation from Maine to California? Why are scores of Black folk once again asking the question, "Can we finally just be called American and not African American?"

Without a doubt, we have good reason to celebrate a lived hope in the inauguration of President Obama. Some things have changed, and progress has been made. But we should not forget "the stony road we trod, bitter the chastening rod, felt in the days when hope unborn had died." Race, color, and gender prejudices have not been completely overcome. African American lives have been (and in some quadrants continue to be) traumatized by a nation that has sought to work out its own identity issues and series of crises through segregation, subjugation, and racial terrorism.

Although we continue to live with the vestiges of racial injustice, the old image of manhood is not completely adequate for molding African American manhood for today and tomorrow. We must encourage African American men to maintain the resistance that has kept us alive and loving life for more than four hundred years. The soil cries out with the blood of thousands of men and women who were brutalized and died resisting degradation. To silence their voices and continue to deny that we are not our brothers' and sisters' keepers is to diminish their testimonies, overlook their sacrifices, and condemn the community to extinction by our refusal to take responsibility in life. We have survived as a people because we understood in the core of our being that if one of us was going to make it, all of us would have to make it! To surrender that hope is to surrender to the principalities and powers that seek to devour our flesh.

Post–Civil Rights, Not Post–Human Rights

Although we are in a post–Civil Rights era, I do not believe we are in a postracial era or a post–human rights era. Color, sex, and gender still define humanity. In order to combat the negative forces from without and within the African American community, we must reaffirm the importance of fatherhood to community development. This, of course, is not intended to suggest fatherhood is the most important feature of community life. We have survived as a people and community because men and women, young and old, have all committed to work to resist the beast that would devour our souls. If we men, however, will not step up to take responsibility for our manhood and the community, we will sacrifice both and gain nothing. I am promoting the revision of extended fatherhood as a way of encouraging men to become more responsible and nurturing as men. Mentoring, an important feature of extended fatherhood, is essential to the overall health of the community. Because we have been so image oriented in our development as community leaders, I want to encourage us to reflect on appropriate images for the future.

The dominant images of the post–Civil Rights struggle can be seen in the contemporary positions held by men like Doctors Cornel West and Michael Dyson, Minister Louis Farrakhan, and former secretary of state Colin Powell. They are all cultural critics who lead, guide, and advocate responsibility without sacrificing the complexity and integrity of African American life. There are also social icons like Morgan Freeman, Denzel Washington, Tavis Smiley, and Tupac who each represent how our work positions us within society. Through our work, we can set the tone and model the respect we still long for and deserve. Our long history of having been disrespected continues to cry out for justice and the images of status and success.

Beyond identifying specific men who embody the classic images as well as promote new concerns for all to see today, the iconic images of the African warrior, the Buffalo soldier, the Tuskegee airman, and the Black Panther all inspire pride, courage, integrity, and guardianship as they represent and defend the community. The iconic image of the African American father holding his child in a nurturing embrace is also becoming more popular and com-

128

monplace in art and marketing media. All these images encourage men to act responsibly on behalf of and for the benefit of the African American community.

Biblical Character Study

To explore these dynamics, let us reconsider the character of manhood by reflecting on 1 Timothy 3. This Pauline letter focuses on the important attributes for the offices of bishop and deacon. Paul notes that if any man desires one of these offices, there are particular attitudes, qualities, and ways of living that a man must embody. These offices are positions of honor, responsibility, and respect within the community. Although I am not suggesting that every man needs to desire the office of bishop or deacon, I am suggesting that the model of manhood that exemplifies the best of what Paul described are the characteristics and attributes of a community leader. For us, Paul suggests that to desire to be a community leader is to desire to do good work among the people.

All of the attributes identified in this letter are related to a man's public and private life. A man's integrity must be constant and consistent. He cannot be responsible in his public life and irresponsible in his private life. As a leader, a man's good reputation should always precede him. He must be generous with what he has and welcoming even when he has nothing. Because the well-being of the family and the community are high priorities, he remains vigilant to address the needs of everyone he meets. He remains sober in his judgments, not given to the fanciful when practicality is needed. He is generative—that is, he always desires to mentor the next generation and to give them good gifts for living.

When manhood is grounded in extended fatherhood as the model of leadership, a man's work to bring change and transformation to community life is a spiritual witness of courage. For him violence is not a first response but a last resort. As Ecclesiastes declares, "There is a season, and a time for every matter under heaven.... [There is] a time for war, and a time for peace." There are times when we must fight—and perhaps even die—to protect those we love. A leader is not motivated by greed, which promotes personal gain; rather, he is motivated by initiatives that promote a community's self-determination and revitalization. He understands very well that nurturing dignity requires patience, long-suffering, and faith.

By grace, let us not end this conversation. Let's continue to talk openly and honestly with one another as we strive to become the men we have always hoped to be.

Notes

4. Not My Son

1. The cases in this chapter are compiled from interviews and conversations with and about heterosexual and gay fathers and their gay sons.

2. In a 2002 essay, I included my mother's use of the term *all-boy* in a positive reference to my heterosexual brother. See "Black Machoism and Its Discontents" in *Face to Face: A Discussion of Critical Issues in Pastoral Theology.*

3. The psychoanalyst Sigmund Freud asserted that male homosexuality existed as a result of a domineering mother and distant father.

4. *Living Human Document* is a term coined by pastoral theologian Anton Boisen, referring to the stories that individuals reveal from their experience.

5. It's a . . . Girl

1. An egalitarian role expectation is the desire for men and women to share equally in the rearing of children as well as sharing the work tasks within the home. An androgynous role expectation is related to the male or female performing both the provider role and the nurturing role without regard to traditional gender role expectations.

2. Faustina E. Haynes, "Gender and Family Ideals: An Exploratory Study of Black Middle-Class Americans," *Journal of Family Issues* (October 2000): 834.

3. Ibid., 811-37.

4. Bernard Kynes, "African American Fathers as Caregivers" (Atlanta: Unpublished paper, Georgia Association of Pastoral Care and Counseling, 2001).

5. Edward P. Wimberly, *Counseling African American Marriages and Families* (Westminster/John Knox, 1997), 70.

6. Bethany L. Letiecq and Sally A. Koblinsky, "Parenting in Violent Neighborhoods: African American Fathers Share Strategies for Keeping Children Safe," *Journal of Family Issues* (September 2004): 715-34.

7. Carolyn A. Smith, et al., "African American Fathers: Myths and Realities about Their Involvement with Their Firstborn Children," *Journal of Family Issues* (October 2005): 996.

8. Kynes, "African American Fathers as Caregivers," 7.

6. Daddy's Little Girl

1. See Jonetta Rose Barras, *Whatever Happened to Daddy's Little Girl? The Impact of Fatherlessness on Black Women* (New York: The Ballantine Publishing Group, 2000); and Bebe Moore Campbell, *Sweet Summer: Growing Up with and without My Dad* (New York: G. P. Putnam's Sons, 1989).

2. Gloria Wade-Gayles, *Father Songs: Testimonies by African-American Sons and Daughters* (Boston: Beacon Press, 1997).

3. *Turning the Corner on Father Absence in Black America: A Statement from the Morehouse Conference on African American Fathers* (Atlanta: Morehouse Research Institute and Institute for American Values, 1999).

4. Houston A. Baker Jr., *Critical Memory: Public Spheres, African American Writing, and Black Fathers and Sons in America* (Athens: University of Georgia Press, 2001); John Edgar Wideman, *Fatheralong: A Meditation on Fathers and Sons, Race and Society* (New York: Pantheon Books, 1994).

5. Barras, *Daddy's Little Girl*, 4.

6. Ibid., 6.

7. Ibid., 24.

8. Ibid., 23-24.

9. Ibid., 24-25.

10. Edward P. Wimberly, *Relational Refugees: Alienation and Reincorporation in African American Churches and Communities* (Nashville: Abingdon, 2000).

11. Flora Wilson Bridges, "A Seat at the Welcome Table," in Wade-Gayles, 168.

12. Nancy Chodorow, *The Reproduction of Mothering: Psychoanalysis and the Sociology of Gender* (Berkeley: University of California Press, 1978).

13. Orlando Patterson, *Rituals of Blood: Consequences of Slavery in Two American Centuries* (Washington, DC: Civitas, 1998).